WALK
WITH A
PURPOSE

THE JOHN VOLKEN STORY
From Dishwasher to Multi-Millionaire,
Then Gave It All Away...

With great warmth and wit, *Walk With a Purpose* tells the story of one man's determined quest to serve God and his fellow men by doing as much good as possible in this world.

◆ FriesenPress

Suite 300 - 990 Fort St
Victoria, BC, V8V 3K2
Canada

www.friesenpress.com

ISBN
978-1-5255-8320-9 (Hardcover)
978-1-5255-8319-3 (Paperback)
978-1-5255-8321-6 (eBook)

1. BIOGRAPHY & AUTOBIOGRAPHY, BUSINESS

Distributed to the trade by The Ingram Book
Company

Cover Design by Nicole Bonilla

All proceeds from this
book go to charity.

TABLE OF CONTENTS

THANK YOU!
ACKNOWLEDGEMENTS

When I think of all the people who influenced my life and helped me along the way, I would need a separate book to acknowledge each of them. So, if you feel left out—you are never forgotten.

But my wife is the one who is in the forefront of my mind. Daily, I am reminded how blessed I am by her, my best friend and wife, Chawna. You amaze me with your dedication, discernment, intelligence, beauty, and love. Thank you for being on this adventure with me . . .

And thanks for your mother Charlene and stepfather Mel, together with your eight siblings, who so warmly welcomed me as part of your awesome family. I'm not surprised that in 1984 your family was invited to the White House to be honored as the "Family of the Year."

And how can I not mention Chawna's brother, my friend Carson, who almost daily stimulates me with humour and sound advice. He was also instrumental in establishing the John Volken Academy in Arizona. I am part of an amazing family!

Over the years, many people, especially parents of the John Volken Academy students, have encouraged me to write about my life—to tell why I do what I do. Thank you for your confidence that I could accomplish such a feat. However, much of the book was first written by a "ghost" writer, followed by my rewriting it, keeping the main narrative. My secretary Jane Terepocki constantly typed and retyped my writing. Then, it was partly edited by my sister-in-law Jennifer Brown, who also was involved in selecting the title for this book. Bilhar Koonar, David Berner, Susan Richards de Wit, and others contributed to the writing. Thank you all! You know I could not have done it without you.

I was blessed with an exceptional father. He made the ultimate sacrifice for his country—and did so willingly. He left a legacy of commitment, loyalty, and courage among many other values . . . and I am so grateful for my mother who alone, with three small boys, crawled through those early years after World War II—successfully. Blessed is the son who feels that way about his parents. Thank you for your examples.

Much love goes to my three children: Uve, Lisanne, and Talia, who taught me what "a father's love" is all about. And to their mother, who taught me that time can heal all wounds. Love as well to my wife Chawna's five children, who adopted me . . . and my five grandchildren, who remind me that being a grandfather has little to do with age.

Love and thanks to my two brothers, Roger and Bernd, who taught me that blood is thicker than water.

I benefited greatly from my many childhood friends—especially Peter, Hartmut, and Klaus. These friendships grew from building forts in the woods as youngsters, to afford me a sense of security, even when we, as adults, were an ocean apart.

Thanks to my old friend James Gans, who taught me forgiveness and instilled in me a strong sense of humanity.

Thanks to my bosses early in life, who built my confidence when they appreciated my performance.

Thanks to my many friends along the way in Markham, Ontario; North Bay, Ontario; Montreal, Quebec; Las Vegas, Nevada; and now in Kent, WA; Gilbert, AZ; and Vancouver, BC. You know who you are. You blessed my life with encouragement, security, smiles, and well-being. Thank you.

I am indebted to the many thousands of my employees over the years. Without you I could have never built the businesses that finance the Lift the Children Charity in Africa and the John Volken Academy in North America. Thank you for your many years of loyal service, especially Randy Klotz, who has worked with me for thirty-five years; Doran Pierson for thirty years; and my friend and legal advisor Bilhar Koonar for twenty-five years.

Cordell Rolfson, David Litchfield, Don Ream, Mel Stradling, Seth Keeler, Tom Walker…and so many others. Your exceptional examples of humility and spirituality continuously inspire me to strive for a higher plane. I will forever be grateful for your role in my sojourn here on earth.

I am grateful to the many selfless individuals everywhere who give so much of themselves to make this world a better place with no expectation of any reward. It is humbling, and their actions prompt me to do better.

A special nod of gratitude to President Ronald Reagan and to the Duke, John Wayne, for epitomizing the United States I love.

Where would the John Volken Academy be without the actions of my friends Carole Mikita, Abdul Ladha, Dr. Joseph Segal, and Kyle McKay? Your individual actions have impacted the advancement of the John Volken Academy (JVA) immeasurably . . . and my friends Conley Wolfswinkel and Rick Diamond for your continued support. You have my lasting gratitude.

With love and respect I think of each student of the John Volken Academy as they strive to become the best that they can be, along with the many graduates who are now contributing members of society. Your changes are inspiring and will have an impact on generations to come. And to the devotion of the John Volken Academy staff who makes it all possible, together with parents and loved ones who encourage the struggling students in the quest for sobriety—thank you so much.

Thank you as well to the many advisory committee members in Arizona, Washington, and British Columbia, and the volunteers who so effectively and selflessly dedicate their time and talents to advancing the John Volken

Academy and Lift the Children. A book could be written about your many contributions. Where would the John Volken Academy and Lift the Children be without you? My heart is filled with gratitude.

And finally, the source of influence and guidance is undeniable. I am thinking of my time at the orphanage as a youngster. Instead of unhappy, even hurtful memories that often accompany the thoughts of an orphanage, I have only fond memories. Then I recall: the immigration to Canada and the ease in amassing a fortune and viewing the money as a stewardship rather than an ownership; the natural transition to use the funds to organize and maintain Lift the Children in Africa and the John Volken Academy in the US and Canada; the constant decisions required to run these charities for which I am clearly not able to take credit. In humility and thankfulness, I place it all on the altar of my God. I only hope to live up to the privilege. My gratitude is eternal.

CHAPTER 1

CAPTURED BY THE WHIRLWIND
Reinvention Has Been a Lifetime Companion

On a late June morning in 2017, Roy Anderson, a senior student at the John Volken Academy is giving a potential new student and his mother a tour of the campus in Surrey, BC, when the three of them bump into John Volken. Introductions are made and the young man's mother expresses her hope that her heroin-addicted son will sign up.

Her son, averting his eyes says, "I have to think about it."

John asks, "What will you think about?"

He replies, "It's . . . what? Two years?"

With Anderson nodding, John says, "That's what it takes. That's how long it takes to heal your addictive mind and learn a healthy new lifestyle that will keep you sober . . . in fact, it may take up to five years for the brain to get as good as it can be."

"I have to think about it," the young man says, now looking at his mother whose frustrated expression seems to say, *I've heard this before.*

Anderson agrees, "It is rigorous. Changing your life is challenging, and furthermore, inductees are not allowed any contact with family or friends for the first month."

The young man asks, "I can't see my friends . . . at all?"

"No. Nobody for the first month."

"Jeez."

"After that," adds Anderson, "you get letters and phone calls and more privileges as you progress through the program."

Again: "Jeez. That's hard! I've gotta think about it. I can try to stop (using heroin) myself," he suggests to his mother.

She tells him, "You've said that before."

John asks the young man, "Didn't work, right?"

"Right," he agrees.

"To be accepted into the program, you have to be committed to changing your life," John says. He warmly bids the mother and her son goodbye, encouraging them to consider taking this step.

Changing one's life is challenging. John Volken knows this well. Reinvention has been a lifetime companion. In 1955, at age fourteen, Volker Jahn (his birth name) fled Russian-occupied East Germany by himself to seek freedom and opportunities in West Germany.

In September 1960, at eighteen years old, he arrived in Canada. He found himself sleeping on a bench in a Toronto railway station with less than ninety dollars in his pocket and a loaf of Wonder Bread for his supper. He spoke no English (in East Germany he had learned Russian) and had no particular job skills, but he was blessed with hope, ambition, and a penchant for hard work. Unemployment was high at the time, and he appreciated it when a farmer let him stay at his farm through the winter. Hard work, no pay, but food and a bed. John was happy. The next step was washing dishes . . . and eventually, in 1981, he started with one little second-hand store and built it to become one of the largest furniture chains in North America with 151 stores.

He sold the company in 2003 and gave the proceeds away by transferring the real estate holdings and other assets to the two John Volken Foundations to support his charitable endeavors.

Today, John resides on the Surrey academy's campus. Unlike most philanthropists, he is a hands-on benefactor. His days are spent doing the myriad tasks—small and large—that are required to run one of the most revolutionary and successful therapeutic communities in North America.

He lives with his philosophy and its daily application. Running meetings. Managing staff. Teaching classes. Dealing with students' frustrations and fears. Serving as a model for how to embrace change and opportunity.

Much can be said about John, but the best way to get to know him is to follow him around as he accomplishes his daily tasks to get a closer look into what he's really about.

"Hi," he says to a young man who's offering fresh-out-of-the-oven cookies at the PricePro entrance. PricePro is a vast supermarket that's also a training facility for JVA students recovering from their addictions. "How's it going?"

"Oh, not too bad."

"Sorry to hear that. How can I help?" John replies. The young man, somewhat puzzled, tells him he is all right. John uses it as a teaching opportunity. 'Not too bad'—what you are saying is you are bad . . . but not too bad. The answer should be, 'I am all right or I am fine . . . (and tomorrow I'll be even better')." From this exchange the young man learns that language is important.

John takes stairs two-at-a-time, ducks into the PricePro offices for a quick chat with the accountant, then heads back down the stairs, greeting other JVA students working as cashiers and clerks with his familiar, "How's it going?" Up the back stairs now—again two-at-a-time. Nothing in John Volken's world, the trailing visitor observes, is slow.

Above the PricePro supermarket are offices, including those of John's lawyer and secretary, the boardroom, and John's apartment. There are wall-mounted, framed newspaper clippings of him opening one of his United Furniture Warehouse stores, and nearby is a *BC Magazine* cover of him being declared 1995 Entrepreneur of the Year. Farther down the hall is his office, which is filled with addiction-recovery books, files of individual students, and letters from grateful parents and recovering addicts. Before you get to the door to the sprawling apartment he shares with his wife, Chawna, there's a constellation of family and historic images. These reveal, in John's verbal captioning, his Prussian roots; his family tree; and a golden icon of one of his heroes, Saint Francis of Assisi. Years ago, John says, it was in the town of Assisi, Italy, that he received spiritual confirmation of his plan to redirect his wealth and minister to the world's troubled and suffering brothers and sisters. That plan—to build a place where addicts can escape their demons while they learn life skills, and to help them become the best that they can be—is now a reality.

The whirlwind tour of the academy and its campus ends upstairs in The Africa Room, where framed photographs of African orphanages cover the walls. John founded Lift the Children in 2009 and continues to support fifty-four of Kenya and Uganda's orphanages, which protect and sustain thousands of African children. Some of these children are in the photos that line one wall of the meeting room. The young boys' heads are shaved. The young girls' hairdos are often beaded with colored baubles. And there are photographs like John standing amid a jammed cluster of cheery and healthy children. He stands tall among them, white-haired and tanned, wearing a khaki shirt. He seems grateful to be able to help.

John has brought along a few albums from his collection of photos, to prompt his memory as to how all of this came about. Where did it all begin? What were the critical, pivoting moments where insight or momentum, defeat or wanderlust, propelled him to seek new opportunities?

Sitting down at last, he opens the first album, full of black-and-white photographs taken in post-war Germany, and begins telling a remarkable story.

CHAPTER 2

THE LITTLE RASCAL
Rebellion and Restlessness in Post-War Germany

As John Volken opens the first of his stack of photo albums, each page shows images of the boy he once was. Born during World War II in East (communist) Germany, he was raised by a widowed mother, schooled in Marxist-Leninist principles, and dreamed of adventures far beyond his homeland. Black-and-white photos show his mother's ancestors, members of the Prussian gentry dressed in early-twentieth-century, ankle-length satin skirts and tailored morning suits. His father is in his German uniform with an insignia that indicates he's a doctor, not a soldier. A mischievous-looking, eleven-year-old John stands with his brothers, Rüdiger and Bernhard, before their Arnstadt apartment with their mother, looking out an open window just above them. The images hardly suggest the man he would eventually become.

Another page shows the orphanage he lived in when he was ten. There is the town of Arnstadt with its cobblestone streets, medieval, red-tile-roofed buildings, and a picture of his cousin's dachshund, Lumpi. There is the Bach Church where a young Johann Sebastian played the organ and was dismissed in 1707 for kissing a girl in the organ loft. "He was a rascal, too," John says with a meaningful laugh.

As the album's pages are turned and the stories that the photos evoke are gradually told, the reasons for John's use of the word "too" becomes clear. His mother often called him *Kleiner Schlingel*—little rascal. He was then and has been since, a person who defied convention and took risks.

As his mother said of him shortly before that day in 1960 when he left Germany for Canada, "He's like a cat. Whatever happens to him, he'll always land on his feet."

John Volken was actually christened as Volker Jahn, but reversed and respelled his name in Canada. In December 1941, the little Volker was born in Potsdam, the old capital of Prussian Germany. This is where his eventual political hero, Frederick II, or Frederick the Great, ruled in the mid-eighteenth century.

In one of John's albums is a photo of the castle where Frederick II was imprisoned—by his own father. As a young man, Frederick had tried to flee the strict Prussian court for the pleasures of Holland. On John's apartment wall hangs an etching of Frederick II. "He's one of my all-time heroes. Very Prussian. Strict but fair. He was way ahead of his time. As absolute ruler he lived by the motto, 'I'm the first servant of my country.'"

In early 1942, the Jahn family moved to Meinberg, a small town in Eastern Germany. John's father, Rudolf, was a young doctor who had met his wife (Lisanne, nee Preussmann, which translates to Prussian Man), a nurse, just prior to the outbreak of World War II. For a while, Rudolf practiced as a local doctor in and around Meinberg. But in 1944, as Germany's Eastern Front against the Soviet forces collapsed, he announced to his wife, "I have to enlist. It is my duty. When the war is over and my children ask me, 'Dad, where were you when Germany was burning?' I cannot face them and say I was at home."

John focuses on the last photograph of his father, taken in 1944. He stands in uniform in his Meinberg home with his wife and three young sons. "I get emotional when I think about it," says John. "He volunteered and was sent to Denmark, then Russia, and eventually died in Poland in February 1945, just before the war's end. My mother talked a lot about him and tried to instill in us three boys some of his qualities. He was strict and strong in his convictions. He was an idealist. I am proud of my father. My mother heard about his death in a hand-delivered letter from German military officials. His body was never found."

By the spring of 1945, the German Army had collapsed, and Soviet forces occupied Meinberg. Their sudden appearance forms some of the first memories, not surprisingly, of the three-year-old John. He remembers seeking refuge in the basement when horse-mounted Russian soldiers went galloping by the basement window. His mother was often out securing food for her family from his dad's former patients at nearby farms. During one such time, John saw Soviet trucks disgorge soldiers, who scattered through the neighborhood. Terrified, the three boys hid in a neighbor's potato cellar until they were found by their very worried mother. He also recalls a Russian officer sitting in the family living room on the rocking horse, pretending to ride it as he chatted with his mother. It was a calming sight for young John. "Looking back, I think we were very lucky."

The economic and social upheaval that followed the war's end in 1945 forced millions of Germans into destitution, hunger, wandering, and grief. More than four million German soldiers had died. Many of the country's cities were in ruins, as were its industries. The basic necessities were scarce. Into this vacuum flowed the two victorious armies: Allied military controlled the west—Soviet military the east.

Faced with the death of her husband and little in the way of food or support in Meinberg, John's mother moved her children to Arnstadt, a 1,300-year-old city of half-timbered homes and medieval castles on the edge of the mountainous Thuringia Forest. His mother had lived there as a girl, and his grandmother still lived there along with some of her grown children. And it is there that John grew up, among aunts and uncles and cousins. Even though Arnstadt lay within the Russian-occupied zone, John's memories of those childhood years are often happy. At Easter, his mother would take Easter eggs into the nearby woods, and her sons would then race about madly trying to find them. He bicycled, chased girls with nettle branches, had snowball fights, collected blueberries in the forest, built forts, and went camping. There were weekends spent visiting the family orchards and vegetable gardens, but most exciting to him was just spending time with friends.

"Looking back," says John. "I enjoyed my childhood. We did without, but we didn't know any different. And not having a dad was not unique.

As a child I never really missed my father because I didn't remember him. Among my close friends, nobody had a father. That was the German way after the war. We grew up, and it was always: mother, mother, mother. Family members told stories about how exceptional my father was. Tall and handsome, intelligent, an idealist, athletic, sober, loving of his wife and children, and hardworking. He went back to university to become a medical doctor after having a career at the Post Office, like his father who died in the First World War. I often thought about that, and it gave me, and still does, a sense of security, pride, and love."

Reflecting on the consequences of growing up fatherless, John says he suspects that it has subconsciously affected him. "It seems like I've always been drawn to older men in a respectful or admiring way. I'd listen to them. I'd remember their stories. They always left an impression on me. I've learned that's what happens when you grow up without a father; you often reach out to father figures."

In 1950, nine-year-old John and his older brother, Bernd, were sent to an orphanage in nearby Eisenach for ten months while his mother was hospitalized. He recalls the time with great fondness, because, despite missing his mother, he and the other boys could be rowdy—jumping on beds, fighting, exploring the neighborhood forest, and on occasion, irritating the nurse tasked to control thirty rambunctious and parentless boys. And there was always enough food, a high priority to a growing boy. He remembers the youthful camaraderie, the mischief, the weekend outings in the Thuringia Forest, and the steep climbs to the ridge-top, twelfth-century Wartburg Castle. In the early sixteenth century, Martin Luther had translated the Bible into German there, thus laying the foundation of a unified German language and beginning the Protestants' insurgence.

"As a child, living in an orphanage made a lasting impression on me," John says. "Without a doubt, being at an orphanage was instrumental to what I am doing today."

The roots of John's attitudes toward achievement, politics, money, spiritual matters, and rebelliousness were all apparent even during these formative years between 1946 and 1955 in Soviet-occupied East Germany (formally the German Democratic Republic). He recalls his loving but strict mother doing her best to act as both mother and father to her energetic, often misbehaving sons. He remembers early-morning market trips where they'd stand in long queues for meat or vegetables or eggs, only to discover the shops had sold out their stock. He recalls meals of pan-fried potatoes and mashed cabbage—and sometimes little else. He recalls regularly going to a Lutheran church in Arnstadt and finding in the quiet and spiritual atmosphere a deep sense of comfort. And he recalls forest walks with his family, where they would collect loads of pine cones to burn in their old-fashioned stove in the winter.

In elementary school, his athletic prowess was sufficient to earn him the nickname *Schnelles Reh*, translated into English as Quick Deer. He was a stand-out student, whose grades were exceptional, and so were his leadership abilities. In grade five, he led his class in a citywide competition to collect the most scrap metal for recycling. He hounded his classmates to volunteer and led convoys into Arnstadt neighborhoods, soliciting any metal they could scrounge from auto repair shops, homes, and factories. Under John's leadership, his class won the competition.

He also displayed entrepreneurial leadership in seeking out and collecting special wild herbs to be used for medical purposes. He swept sidewalks without being asked and collected snails for export to France to be consumed as escargots. However, his enthusiasm was somewhat tempered when he stored a large pail of snails in his home's foyer to be taken to school the next morning. The snails, not wanting to be confined in the pail, "escaped" overnight, leaving tracks all over the walls. The walls were covered with satin material, and even young John could see that it was a disaster. From this, he learned that enthusiasm without plans may end up in disappointment.

As the years of the early 1950s passed, the freedom and economic recovery of West Germany only served to magnify the differences between that and the political depression and economic disaster of the world in which John lived. At this time he began to display some of the independence and adolescent rebelliousness that would propel him first to West Germany, and then—four years later—across the Atlantic to Canada.

Despite being an excellent student who was popular among his class-mates, John was always a bit of a rebel and occasionally behaved recklessly. He once risked expulsion for an act that challenged school authorities, and in another instance could have blown up his school.

He was living with his uncle, aunt, and cousin Juergen during most of 1952. Juergen was a few years younger, and an only child, so John became somewhat of a brother to him. Like his dad, he became a dentist and retired in 2005. Their relationship continues to be close to this day.

While John was regularly getting into trouble for small infractions of school rules, his aunt warned him that his continuous rule breaking was not acceptable. If he got a three in behavior on his report card, she said, he'd be in deep trouble. The country's educational grading system ran from one (excellent) to three (passing) to five (bad). And he suspected his aunt's edict might well be an accurate assessment of where he was headed. After class one day, when he was the last kid in the room, he opened the teacher's grading book, and there beside his name were ones and twos for various academic achievements, but beside behavior was a three. He knew he was in trouble. So he took the book—with all the students' grades—put it in his school bag, ran home, and buried it in the compost pile.

He'd told his best friend what he'd done, but his friend couldn't believe it.

John said, "Yeah, I did." His friend promised that he wouldn't tell. Soon though, the police got involved and John was questioned.

> I was ten years old and scared when they took out a pair of handcuffs. I thought perhaps my friend had "betrayed" me so I'd better tell the truth. I took them to the compost pile and dug up the book. It was all covered in dirt and garbage when I handed it to them.
>
> My uncle told me, "If we had a place to send you, we'd send you there." He was a well-educated man, a dentist with an impeccable reputation. He didn't need a family member to embarrass him.
>
> They never did send me away. In fact, when I needed a German sponsor to be accepted into Canada, my uncle wrote a glowing letter about me. Of course, that was

about seven years after the "deed," and I was reluctantly
on the straight and narrow.

However, where I'd had a three in the grade book seven
years previously, I got a five for behavior that year.

Lesson learned.

If hiding his class's grade book was a serious, but relatively harmless infraction, his actions in the school chemistry lab about a year later could have been disastrous. At the end of the class, he turned on the Bunsen burner in the chemistry lab, and gas escaped all night long. It was discovered the next morning, and the entire class was confronted by the principal, who asked, "Who did that? The whole school could have been blown up."

"It was one of those scary moments," says John. "My classmates talked me into not telling—they thought it was cool." And because no one confessed, the teacher insisted that everyone stay after school and line up adjacent to the classroom door, until someone confessed. John, standing first in line by the door, passed a whispered message down the line of boys, saying, "When the buzzer rings for school to end, everyone rush out."

So, when the buzzer rang, John was the first to split. A few boys followed until the teacher stopped the rest from leaving. Because John had been the leader in leaving when the bell rang, his mother was called to come to school the next day to explain her son's disrespect to authorities. The gas leak was never mentioned.

"I always pushed the envelope, and it seems I mostly got away with things. Those experiences help me today to not judge our students. There is a light in all of us."

He reflects on another of his youthful escapades in East Germany when he stole cigarettes from his mother's front-door stash. They were meant for tipping the postman or deliverymen—no one in the Volken household smoked. John led about twenty of his grade-four buddies into the woods for an illicit, first-ever smoke. He broke the cigarettes into thirds, passed the stubs around, and lit them. His buddies, all excited, inhaled the tobacco and immediately began coughing, but they could still bring themselves to say, "This is fun."

In his retelling, John laughingly mimics the ensuing eruption of hacking sounds. "Then it was finally my turn, and I simply said, 'This is stupid. I'm never going to smoke. Just look at you . . . this isn't fun.' As I announced that I was never going to smoke, most of my buddies said, 'Neither will I,' and threw the cigarette butts to the ground. This was one of my most valuable life lessons . . . namely to always follow my own gut instincts or inner compass, often swimming upstream, bucking conventional wisdom, and never going with the crowd. In general, that has served me well."

And in the same way, as an adult, he listened to "experienced" people in any field, but ultimately made decisions based on his own instincts. He has been called stubborn. He is okay with that.

That kind of thinking or "pushing the envelope" is still part of John. Recently, when crossing the border between Canada and the United States by car, he and his wife Chawna were on a side street, waiting to enter the main road to the border. Their lineup was at a dead stop, and John went to investigate. About twenty cars ahead was a lady, obviously frustrated because no one would let her into the main line. So, John stepped into the main road, stopped the cars, and let all the side street's cars in—on an alternating basis. While the "side street cars" cheered him on, the ones he stopped on the main road wanted to run him over—they were furious.

Or, on his last trip visiting his brother in Germany, he got dizzy and couldn't get up, so Chawna and his brother Bernhard took him to the hospital. The nurse put him on an intravenous and cardiac monitor and told him that it could be serious. His limited motion pointed to a possible stroke, and his loved ones were genuinely concerned. When John told the doctor that he was expected in another city the next day, the doctor wanted no part of it and insisted his patient stay at least another day for observation.

Well, by early morning, John felt a lot better and could walk without the walker. He disconnected the intravenous and the cords to the monitor and went down the corridor towards the exit . . . with cords and part of his IV hanging out. His wife and brother had just arrived to check up on him, and John greeted them with, "Let's get out of here."

Outside the hospital, to the dismay of his brother and wife, he removed the bandage, the IV needle, and the plugs of the monitor. Despite the strong protests of his family, he insisted they all continue to leave. There were some follow-up consequences to his "escape" from the hospital, but a day was saved and in the end, all was well.

Stories like that seem to follow John—he always wants to get to the bottom line with as little delay as possible. It has served him well to this day, but especially during his business career.

In the spring of 1955, John was in grade eight. He remembers the day the principal came into his class and said to all the boys, "Those who want to go to high school, please stand." John hadn't exactly thought much about what he wanted to do. Life in East Germany was oppressive, but he also knew that not advancing his education would mean the end of his public schooling. Government regulations at that time forced most fourteen-year-olds into jobs after grade eight. He stood up, along with some friends.

"All those who stood up," John reports, "were denied high school. And some of the ones who didn't stand were coerced into going to high school. It was political. The regime wanted to educate the children of blue-collar workers because they would be more inclined to embrace the ruling regime . . . the best chance for future communists."

In West Germany, an association of medical doctors was paying for vacation time for young teenagers to visit. John was one of the lucky ones. So in September 1955, he climbed onto an East German train on the way to West Germany. The wall separating East and West Germany wouldn't be built until the early 1960s. Today, John revels in the memory of first crossing the border between East and West. It was emotional. Even as a fourteen-year-old, he understood "freedom."

During his two-week vacation in West Germany, he decided not to go back home. "I was fourteen years old and needed my mother's permission, and I was surprised by her response. I thought she'd want me back—I was a child. But she encouraged me in my decision with, 'There's no future for you in East Germany.' She always had confidence in me. I am grateful for that."

In West Germany he was on his own and needed a place that offered room and board. He found the ideal situation—working and living on a farm. His work was mostly around pigs, and he learned to admire the personalities and intelligence of those animals. The following spring he started a three-year apprenticeship in Bardowick, a village just southeast of Hamburg, with the intention of becoming a gardener. He always enjoyed nature, and gardening was the closest thing to it. He worked in greenhouses, learning about flowers and bulbs and floral products. As a child, he fantasized about becoming the captain of a ship and seeing the world, but more realistically about becoming a forest ranger or farmer. Working with the earth and nature was in his DNA from his mother's side. The three-year apprenticeship as a gardener was fifty-six hours per week, and it paid twenty-two Deutsche Marks per month plus room and board. However, there was always enough time and money to go to night school, take boxing lessons, and date his first girlfriend. Those were busy times, but John reveled in them. Three years later, he graduated as a certified gardener. He never worked as a gardener, but gardening became his lifelong hobby.

In 1958, John's younger brother, Rüdiger, arrived from East Germany. Then a year later, his mother and her eldest son, Bernd, arrived in nearby Lüneburg about twenty miles from where John had done his apprenticeship as a gardener. For a short time, the family was reunited. But by then, John was disenchanted with the prospects of a life growing flowers as a career, and his wanderlust led him to investigate options across the Atlantic. His choice was, of course, the United States. But he quickly learned, with considerable disappointment, that the USA's immigration regulations required having a sponsor and a job offer. He had neither. So, he then began to look elsewhere: To Australia? Or to Canada? At the time, it was a toss-up.

As a boy he'd read about Canada, and like many Germans even today, he found the mythology of the country appealing. It seemed to be a wilderness where woodsmen and Indians roamed and where a man could face the elements and be strong and free. This image, founded on early twentieth-century marketing pitches, appealed to John's romanticism. "I'd read about Canada. It was all about lumberjacks and Indians. So I thought, Well, I suppose I'll go to Canada, buy an axe, and cut down trees."

When he told his family and friends about his emigration plans, he didn't get much support. "You don't speak English." (In school he'd had four years of Russian.) "You are too young." "Canada is not civilized." "You have no money, no marketable trade." He heard it all, but it only made him more determined.

His mother silenced what doubts he had by saying, "You're going to be all right wherever you go."

Undeterred by doubters and bureaucratic impediments, John sought out the Canadian Consulate in Hamburg, told the official about his intent, and heard this welcoming response, "Where in Canada do you want to go?"

"I don't know," he replied.

"How about Edmonton?"

He didn't know where Edmonton was, but that didn't matter much. It was somewhere in the English-speaking part of Canada. So, he agreed, and added, "I don't have any money for the fare."

"That's okay. We'll advance you the fare. You can pay us back when you are able, after you get there." And the official gave him a voucher worth $94 for his trans-Atlantic crossing.

In late-August 1960, John headed for the northern German port of Bremerhaven with his family, who bade him *Auf Wiedersehen*. He climbed aboard the *Seven Seas*, an aging, converted WWII troop ship—along with other immigrants—and set sail for Halifax, Canada, leaving his girlfriend, family, friends, and Germany behind. In his photo album, there's a picture of him, outbound, smiling and leaning against the ship's railing, with longish hair and a preppy white sweater. He looks pleased at the prospects of whatever adventure lies ahead. On the photo, John has written, "Off to Canada, Sept. 1960." He was eighteen.

Two of his fondest expectations of Canada were about to be crushed. During an early shipboard orientation meeting for immigrants, John declared his intention to go to Edmonton. His plan to be a lumberjack was countered with, "Oh, no! You don't want to go there! It's too cold, and what makes you think you'll find a job there?" During that time, Germany's economy was booming, with thousands of foreign workers pouring in to help rebuild the country, which had been destroyed during the war. There was no unemployment. Jobs were plentiful. So young John had that same expectation of Canada.

On the ship he was told, "You don't have to go there. Once you are in Canada, nobody cares where you go. Go to Toronto. That's where the action is, and furthermore, in Canada, they don't chop down trees. They don't use axes. They use chain saws."

With his youthful expectations slightly dampened, he said, "Well then, I'll buy a chain saw." He never did.

Another experience while crossing the Atlantic affected John profoundly. He was in the corner of a shipboard lounge, playing chess with another young German, when an old man walking with a cane approached and stood watching the match. After a while, the man asked, "Do you mind if I play the winner?"

The two young men looked at each other, then looked at the old man, and John said, "Yeah, fine." John won and the old man sat down.

John made some quick assessments about his new opponent: well dressed, seemingly well educated, probably seventy or seventy-five years old.

"So, you're going to Canada?" the man asked. John said he was. The man introduced himself as James Gans and added he was going to Los Angeles but would be heading back to Toronto. If John was there, perhaps they could meet and play some more chess.

John didn't know Gans's story. He didn't know the old man was Jewish. He didn't know what had happened to Gans's family, who'd remained in Germany. Or that Gans had chosen to return to Germany after the war. In fact, he didn't know, when they'd reached Halifax, whether he'd ever see the old man again.

He didn't know that this odd, momentary encounter over a chessboard would have such an impact on the rest of his life.

John Remembers

Growing up in communist East Germany, without a doubt, formed my political opinions. I was just fourteen years old, but very much aware of what Ronald Reagan called "the evil empire."

Political views were suppressed and censored. One had to be very careful about what one said and to whom. Lies published by the government had to be openly accepted and often had to be cheered, or else.

People were arrested for their political views. My father volunteered at the end of the Second World War and died. His brother, like my dad, was a medical doctor, but a high-ranking medical officer. He survived the war but was arrested and never heard from again. We didn't pursue the issue—we didn't dare. Opposing the regime was perilous. Many citizens just disappeared.

Houses were in disrepair because the needed material wasn't available. The more ancient parts of cities collapsed or were razed to the ground. Mere essentials were in short supply, and we had to stand in line for basic food items . . . all this, while the West German free market economy was booming: the *"Wirtschaftswunder"*—the "miracle" economy as it was well- known.

The mood of the population was somber. As children we had our fun. We didn't know better, but I sensed the lack of joy or happiness in the grownups.

During June 1953, rumor had it that workers in East Germany intended to go on strike. I remember Russian tanks rolling all over the city of Erfurt, the capital city of Thuringia, where I lived at the time. During the Hungarian uprising against the Soviet dictatorship in 1956, thousands of Hungarians lost their lives, and the uprising was crushed.

The population of East Germany declined because too many people fled to West Germany (including me). That was the reason why the "Berlin Wall" was built in 1963. And still, people risked their lives, and many were killed trying to escape to West Germany. Imagine risking your life in the quest of leaving your country!

I have always questioned the authorities—I still do. So, all those banners and posters on the streets and in schools trying to convince the citizens that the Soviet Union was fighting for freedom and peace and that they had brought culture to Germany (which was almost funny) had the opposite effect on me. The regime also constantly reminded us that the Soviet Union had liberated the Germans from fascism. That may be true, but it is also true that many people in East Germany thought that fascism was better than the Soviet-Union-imposed communism.

On a lighter note, I fondly remember the Russian soldiers. We often sat with them on the sidewalk and talked. They were very friendly and loved children. However, I detested Stalin's dictatorship or (as I have mentioned previously) what Ronald Reagan called "the Evil Empire." With my family's maternal roots proudly Prussian and from the land-holding class, I sensed the wrongs that were happening in East Germany under Soviet domination. On our classroom walls were large posters that read, "We are thankful for the Soviet people who delivered us from fascism" or "We are fighting for peace," or "Ami go home!"[1] That phrase especially stuck in my mind. We knew that the Americans had helped rebuild West Germany after the war, while the Soviet Union had done the opposite in East Germany.

So, all their propaganda had the opposite effect on me. Everyone understood what the slogan "Ami go home"[1] meant. However, even as a young teenager, to me it meant that if the Soviet/East German regime declared that the

---

1   Yankee Go Home!

"Ami" were the bad guys, then the "Ami" must be the good guys. Logical. That is all I knew about America, and I have loved that country ever since.

Living under socialist/communist rule made me a stout supporter of the free-market system. I believe that supporting and rewarding individual initiatives with minimum interference from government makes us more productive and creates wealth for all. So I am rather conservative in the political and economic sense. And yes, I have a picture of Ronald Reagan in my office. I believe that he and Pope John Paul II were instrumental in bringing down the infamous Berlin Wall.

Challenges and adventures seem to be in my DNA. It prompted me to leave East Germany for West Germany and now I felt the urge to "Go West Young Man." My first choice was the United States, but I needed a sponsor and a job and I had neither. My other options were either Australia or Canada. I chose Canada and never regretted that choice. So in September of 1960 I boarded the Seven Seas in Bremerhaven, Germany on my way to Canada. I was eighteen years old, had less than a hundred dollars, no job and couldn't speak English (I had four years of Russian). Now that was exciting!

1897 My mother's parents
Anna & Arthur Preussmann

1901 My father's parents
Elise & Friedrich Jahn

1922 The Preussmann family. My mother, at 15 years young, is second from left.

1938 My Parents to be.
Rudolf Jahn M.D. and
Lisanne Jahn RN
*   The Perfect Match!*

1942
I was a happy baby,
but when my mother
pinched me, it became
my favourite baby picture.

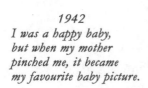

April 1944: Mom & Dad with their three sons. 10 months later the war claimed Dad's life.

CHAPTER 3

GO WEST, YOUNG MAN
Stumbling, Learning, and Succeeding

By the time the Halifax skyline appeared beyond the railing of the *Seven Seas*, the fierce Atlantic storm encountered mid-journey had subsided, the skies had cleared, and the ocean was calm. John considered what lay ahead. He had his wooden trunk with all his belongings but really no idea where he'd end up or what he would do. He'd take the train to Toronto, in the hope of finding a job there. "When I look back," he says, laughing at the memory, "I was young and naïve but with lots of enthusiasm! I knew nobody in Canada. Had ninety dollars. No job. And couldn't speak the language. The only English I knew was a phrase I'd learned on the ship: 'I love you.' My friends said it would one day be useful, but that would have to wait."

John told himself as the ship nosed into its berth, "So, this is it. This is going to be my home and my country. My future."

Despite the challenges ahead, he wasn't worried at all. He didn't know how important it was that he also had the name and contact information for his newfound German acquaintance, James Gans, who'd be staying briefly in Toronto after his trip to Los Angeles. Perhaps they could meet, as Gans had proposed, and carry on their chess playing and conversation later that year.

The following day, John arrived at Toronto's Union Station and recalls thinking, "Well, now what?" Hungry after his westward trip from Nova Scotia, he found a corner store and purchased a memorable loaf of

Wonder Bread. It cost him fifteen cents. Initially he thought, *At that price, I can live for a long time.* But by the next morning, after he had eaten the loaf and slept uneasily on a bench in the train station, the joys of Wonder Bread had diminished, and he sought a real meal at a nearby restaurant's lunch counter.

He studied the menu mounted on the wall above his head, scanning the options, and his eyes settled on the word hamburger. He didn't know what a hamburger was but recognized the word—after all he was German.

Since he didn't speak English, he had to guess that the waitress behind the counter was asking him what he wanted.

"Hamburger," he said, just the way it was pronounced in German.

The waitress seemed puzzled.

He tried a second time: "Hamburger." Again, to no effect.

By coincidence, a woman sitting next to him heard his heavily accented pronunciation. John thought she was an "older woman," but as it turned out she was only twenty-six. (Remember, he was only eighteen.) He recalled later how perceptions change with age.

She asked him in German, "How long have you been in Canada?"

"Since yesterday," he replied.

"Yeah, I can tell." The lady paid for the hamburger and took him to a German friend's Toronto home where he could get fed, sleep, and acquire some advice on work opportunities in and around the city. During the following few days, John was guided around Toronto by his new acquaintances and gradually came to understand that finding a job wasn't as easy in Canada as it was in West Germany. There, the economy was booming with workers coming from all over Europe. At an employment office, he was cautioned that not speaking English was a serious impediment to finding work. "Take any job you can get," they advised.

So his new friends said, "Let's go for a drive." They headed out into the farmland near Toronto, stopping at farms and asking if they needed any help. It was at Lakeview Farm in Stouffville that a Dutch cauliflower farmer said, "I can't pay you, but you can live with us if you are willing to work."

John remembers he was happy: "I had a roof over my head. The next morning, he put me to work in his cauliflower field . . . I tied up the cauliflower heads in their own leaves so they'd stay white. The "ready to be shipped" were put in crates and loaded into a five-ton truck. In the middle of the night—about 3:00 or 4:00 a.m.—we'd drive from Stouffville to the Toronto market where wholesalers bid on produce. So that's what happened every day. It was hard work and long hours. My first job in Canada, and I didn't get paid—I didn't expect to. I was happy. I had food and a place to live, and they were very kind to me. They didn't speak German so I had to learn to communicate in English quickly. Admittedly, I never quite mastered speaking English without an accent—after sixty years!"

As winter descended over Ontario, and the cauliflower harvest was completed, John learned about a job opportunity in nearby Markham—cutting greenhouse daffodils, tulips, and carnations at Markham Florist for the retail flower market. These employers too were Dutch people who didn't speak German, so John improved his English. It paid one dollar an hour. Thought John, *Wow! The first money I've earned in Canada!* He tried to save every penny.

It was at this time that the casual game of chess between an eighteen-year-old young man emigrating to Canada and the elderly German chemist bound for California, James Gans, took a turn that affected much that follows. Gans got word to John that he was staying at the Royal York Hotel in Toronto prior to his departure back to Germany, and that he would be delighted to reconnect if John could visit for a day or two.

The flower farmer drove John to Toronto. He and Gans spent the weekend in long conversations about life and history while touring the city. By the end of that weekend, it seemed Gans had acquired a smart, young friend . . . almost a son he'd never had. And in turn, John had acquired a wise older man as a father figure, which he had never had. Gans asked John to call him James rather than Werner, his preferred Jewish name. They parted but agreed to keep in contact through letters.

By the spring of 1961, John was tired of rural Ontario life and the months living in other people's homes as a guest with people he had no relationship with (he paid six dollars a week for room and board). Having grown up in a mid-sized German town, he decided to find a more urban place where he could settle down for the time being. He looked at a map and decided that the mid-sized town of North Bay would be the place to settle down. North Bay is billed as the Gateway to the North. It lies 350 kilometers (217 miles) north of Toronto on Lake Nipissing.

He had managed to save almost $1,000 from his florist work; enough, he hoped, to provide a grubstake to start a flower shop of his own.

And that's exactly what he did. He rented a small store, nailed shelves to the walls, fixed a curtain across the rear, which provided privacy for his bedroom, and put up a sign that read, "Jahn's Flower Shop." He was nineteen. "With practically no business experience," he says today with an amused laugh. "Just because you like flowers, just because you've worked growing daffodils and tulips, doesn't mean you have any experience running a flower shop."

To start out, he didn't have any flowers. And the nearest flower wholesaler was in Brampton, near Toronto, a four-hour drive south.

He didn't have a vehicle either. Nor did he have a driver's license, not to mention that he didn't know how to drive. But none of these facts appeared to him as insurmountable problems. In North Bay, he found a used, German-made, two-stroke DKW van. In the lingering, late-spring light of a North Bay evening, he set about to quickly teach himself how to drive: clutch down, gearshift pulled, accelerator slightly depressed, clutch released, repeat, repeat, avoid large objects. The following morning, he showed up at the motor vehicle office by himself and announced he wanted to be road-tested. The man asked if he had a car, and he pointed to the empty van beyond the windows. "The natural question from the man might well have been, 'How did you drive here? You don't have a license,'" says John, recounting his memory of that day. "But he didn't say anything. He asked me to drive around the block. We did. Went inside. Filled out the forms. 'Here's your license.' Thank you."

The next day he withdrew all his cash for his purchase of flowers in Brampton. Stopping on the way to buy office supplies for Jahn's Flower Shop, he somehow lost his entire grubstake. Devastated but undeterred, he wired a message to his chess-playing friend, James Gans, and almost immediately got a return message saying Gans had deposited $1,000 in

John's North Bay bank account. So, John drove down the 200 plus miles to Brampton to buy flowers and plants to stock his store.

It didn't take John long to learn that, despite his best hopes and enthusiasm, the flower shop in North Bay was not providing sufficient income to live on. Now what?

He took a night job at a Chinese restaurant, ostensibly as the dishwasher, but actually as a low-paid sous chef, peeling onions and prepping vegetables for the cook until midnight and then cleaning the place. All for twenty-five cents an hour and all the food he could eat. He was tired, but what the heck. There were mornings, when sleeping in the back of his flower shop, John would be awakened by a knocking on the shop's door. But by the time he'd hurriedly dressed, his customer would have departed. This went on for six months before John decided he needed to do something that paid better than trying to sell flowers and peeling onions.

During 1961, John worked on construction. "Nailing tiles on the roof during winter in North Bay was a challenge. It was cold! No gloves and my fingers felt frozen. It's amazing what we can do when we have to."

In late 1962, he took a job as a carpenter at a North Bay trailer factory, even though he knew zero about carpentry except for how to use a hammer. His job was making walls—studs here, plywood there, Arborite down there—that were subsequently assembled into mobile homes. A fulltime job, it paid $1.20 an hour. When a worker was fired, John took over his job, so he ended up doing the work of two, plus cleaning the factory at night. Those were fifteen to sixteen-hour workdays. At breaks and lunch hours he fell asleep. He saved his money, eating mostly carrots at lunch. It saved time because they didn't need preparation. His workmates called him "Bugsy," while John dreamed up grander entrepreneurial schemes. He would use his saved income to get into real estate. Now, he was twenty years old and knew nothing about real estate. His lawyer told him that he wasn't of legal age to own real estate but, "What they don't know won't hurt them."

With rudimentary carpentry skills acquired working on construction and at the trailer factory, he put $500 down on his first North Bay fixer-upper. In time, John became a quick player in the city's low-end real estate market. "I'd buy old, dilapidated houses, fix them up, rent them out, and use the income to pay the mortgages. I had three or four houses on the go at one time—twenty-one altogether. Sometimes I made money. Sometimes I didn't. It was never serious money though. But the experience was priceless. Things always worked out," John says with an attitude he had adopted toward confronting risks and the unknown. "I've learned instinctively to always look for the positive, regardless of how difficult a situation might be. And if we can't find anything positive, even just looking for the positive is positive. If nothing else, it makes one stronger for the next struggle. It's not so much what happens to us, but the attitude—how we react to it."

In the book by Napoleon Hill, *Think & Grow Rich*, John underlined many passages over fifty years ago. One such passage reads, "Life's battles don't always go to the stronger or faster man, but sooner or later, the man who wins is the man *who thinks he can.*" Here is a lesson to be learned.

With a surname that sounded identical to the English name, John, during these first years in Canada John grew tired of explaining that he wasn't John Volker, but Volker Jahn. "People would say, 'What's your name? John?' I'd say, 'Volker Jahn.' Then they'd say, 'What's your last name?' I'd say, 'Jahn.' They'd look confused and ask, 'Your last name's John?' You know, I had to go through that all the time." To make things easier on himself and those he dealt with, he unofficially decided to yield to clarity and reversed his names, adding small spelling changes to become John Volken. He made it official a few years later. (His younger brother, who joined him in North Bay at this time, changed his first name from Rüdiger to Roger to avoid similar problems.)

In the fall of 1963, John received an invitation from Gans to come to Munich that winter and join him on a bus tour through Europe. Gans suggested he and John could continue their chess-playing and philosophical conversations while exploring the continent. It was an offer John couldn't refuse. He spent about one week with family and three weeks touring Europe with his old friend. Among the tourists was a beautiful, eighteen-year-old girl named Maria, whose German father had married a wealthy Mexican woman and was determined to have his daughter acquire the language and knowledge of his Germanic heritage. Soon, Maria and John were sitting together. Maria described the vast Mexican estate her parents owned and the beauty of the land, and suggested, "Wouldn't it be great if you could come to visit Mexico?" They agreed to stay in contact.

It was during this month-long journey around Europe that John heard Gans's complete story. Because of his own German roots, John felt a profound sense of remorse—almost guilt—because what he heard during these conversations would never be forgotten. Gans had been a professor of chemistry at a German university before the Second World War. His father was also a professor and had been a high-ranking officer during the First World War.

Along with millions of other German Jews, Gans could see the writing on the wall. And here is where his amazing story really begins. A former university student of his had become an SS officer, a member of the elite and infamous *Schutzstaffel*. When this former student learned that Gans was about to be arrested, he risked his life and took him on a perilous motorbike ride to safety in neutral Switzerland. From Switzerland, Gans managed to get to Spain, living in obscurity as a chemist until returning to Germany after the war. He was the only member of his family who survived the Holocaust.

Retelling this story over fifty years later, John can barely hold back tears. His voice breaks. "I remember responding, 'If I were you, I could never live in Germany. They killed all your people, your family.' He looked at me and said, 'John, I'm a German.' That response came as a total surprise to me. I thought he would express some negative feeling. Instead, he responded with love and forgiveness. . . I wept. It has been said that the time and place of important, meaningful events will be remembered. This was one of those moments. What a lesson about forgiveness! What a lesson about tolerance! What an exceptional man! I will be forever grateful to be able to call him my friend and mentor."

For five years—until the letters stopped coming—Gans sent John a typewritten letter (and the occasional check) almost every week. In these communications, Gans ruminated on history, philosophy, current events, morality, and much more. John was deeply grateful to have such an insightful confidant. Through Gans's letters to him, John gradually built his own philosophy of acceptance, one that he daily practices today with the often confused and struggling students at the John Volken Academy. "I'll never forget those lessons about forgiveness. Forgiveness is one of the most challenging concepts to deal with. The European Jews were all but wiped out. His whole family was. And yet he somehow managed to overcome that." Gans's stories impacted John's life. "I learned so much from my friend. I can never adequately describe the love and admiration I have for him . . . "

Gans died in 1966, and John still has every letter he received from him more than fifty years ago.

Back in North Bay in 1964, the trailer factory went bankrupt, and John took a job as a salesman at Domestic Foods, an Ottawa-based company that sold freezers stocked with frozen foods. His first week's earnings were $280 and $360 the next week. That was more money than he had made in a month working long hours. And this was fun, talking to people and changing their initial reactions of, "No I don't want it," to "Okay, I'll take it!" To expand his territory, he began heading north—to towns like Temiskaming, Timmins, and Kirkland Lake where the idea proved appealing to people living far from big cities and wide choices. He was twenty-three years old and soon became the company's top salesman. For a while, the money was rolling in. Then, inexplicably, his sales dropped and John became disillusioned with Domestic Foods and commissioned sales.

His sales manager took him aside and offered some sage advice about the nature of sales: "What happens in commissioned sales is that you make good sales, and you're on top of the world. Then your performance drops. You may think your success was a fluke, and you want to quit. But if you keep at it and overcome the setback, you'll be back in the game." John was warned that the same thing would happen about three times. And it did. After that, temporary disappointing sales were just that—temporary. He quickly developed into an accomplished salesman who trained others and helped them to become successful.

As the months passed in North Bay, the size of the town and the limits for adventure started to gnaw on John. He enjoyed his sales job at Domestic Foods and was making $500 to $700 a week—good money in the early 1960s! Even though during any "free" time he was renovating and renting out houses, he was still restless for new challenges.

That restlessness drove him to leave North Bay behind and hit the road, the wanderer off on a new tangent. In 1966, he settled in Montreal and sold life insurance. However, not speaking French was an unassailable barrier to John's being successful in Quebec. Besides, he never really believed in insurance.

Therefore, when he received letters from Maria in Mexico, talking about her wish to be serenaded by him, it created a sort of Romeo and Juliet scenario, which played well to John's youthful, romantic imagination.

So, at the end of October 1966, as winter began closing in over Canada, John told himself, "What the heck! I'm off to Mexico!"

CHAPTER 4

WANDERLUST AND ROMANCE INTERRUPTED
A Journey to Mexico Ends in Las Vegas

During the six years after arriving in Canada, in 1960, John had experienced a life filled with challenges, opportunities, and adventures. He had harvested cauliflower, worked on a tulip farm, and run a flower shop. He'd been a dishwasher, worked in construction, built trailers, bought and sold real estate, sold frozen foods and freezers, and tried his hand at insurance sales. And all the while, he'd acquired the skills of a competent salesman. It came easily to him. But his youthful dreams about journeying to Canada and trying his hand as a north-woods lumberjack never materialized. That would have to wait. A lifelong wanderlust compelled him to move on.

Also, during that time, lay the memory of Maria, the beautiful, German-Mexican young lady he'd met on his Europe trip two years before. He and Maria had been the only youth on an organized bus tour of Germany. The rest of the tourists were elderly, including her German grandmother and John's friend Gans. It was the memory of Maria's invitation that fueled John's ambition to seize the opportunity and find out what a journey of 2,500 miles southwest from Montreal to Mexico might reveal. After all, if this young lady had a boyfriend, he told himself, she wouldn't have invited him. "I didn't so much decide to pursue Maria. I just thought, *Hmm, kind of boring here now, I might as well see what a trip to Mexico will bring.*"

In October 1966, he entrusted most of his belongings to a friend in Montreal, packed his clothing necessities in his blue Volkswagen Beetle, and embarked on a new adventure. Ahead of him on his way to Los Angeles lay Chicago, Illinois; Des Moines, Iowa; and Lincoln, Nebraska, to be followed by the end goal—Mexico.

The cold weather was just ahead, and his Volkswagen had no heater. When he approached Wyoming, a fierce storm hit the area with temperatures far below freezing and almost zero visibility with falling snow. This resulted in him driving off the highway into the lower divide. He immediately stepped on the gas to get back on the road. This quick reaction may well have saved his life. People died in that blizzard. It was one of the many incidents in his life on which he muses about coming close to death. Was this divine intervention or luck?

He checked into a motel in Laramie, Wyoming, where even a hot shower took a while to defrost him. He'd experienced cold working conditions in North Bay, Ontario, and it was, in part, for this reason that Mexico seemed attractive. And well . . . if Mexico didn't work out, he'd head to Vancouver where the winters, he'd heard, were much like those in Germany—never too cold.

The highway carried him farther west to Salt Lake City, Utah, a place first settled in the 1840s by members of The Church of Jesus Christ of Latter-day Saints (LDS). The pioneering, wagon-train-bound religious group had been led by Brigham Young, a follower of its martyred evangelical leader, Joseph Smith.

John's knowledge of Mormonism then was nil, but as it would turn out, this brief encounter with the home of the Mormon religion was a prelude to his conversion from the Lutheran faith to the LDS faith in the years immediately ahead.

Highway 15 South, from Salt Lake City, would have eventually led John to Los Angeles and later to Mexico. But between the two places lay Las Vegas, with all its 1960s neon, glitz, glamour, fancy hotels and cheap motels, all-you-can-eat buffet meals, bouffant hairdos, miniskirts, celebrities, and casinos. What was initially meant to be just a few-days stop in Las Vegas for John, lasted two years. And in time, it changed his life.

It was 1967. It was the year of "If you go to San Francisco," and Haight-Ashbury's famous "Summer of Love." Everywhere in the USA was evidence of westward-drifting hippies, anti-Vietnam War protests, and youthful rebellion. In Canada, it was the year of Expo 67 and the rise of a maverick politician named Pierre Trudeau. But when John Volken rolled into Las Vegas, he saw signs that read: Dean Martin; Frank Sinatra; Red Skelton; Eddie Fisher; the Osmond Family; burlesque's Fabulous Jennie Lee, the Bazoom Girl; and many other personalities. In neon-orange-lit letters, twelve-feet high, a facade on Las Vegas's Fremont Street announced: GOLDEN NUGGET—with the word Saloon above and Gambling Hall below.

"The lights dazzled me for sure. Hotel prices were low! The food was cheap—as low as one-dollar buffets, all-you-can-eat. I checked into the Towne & Country Motel. It's still there. They had a pool, and they charged six dollars a night. And so, I stayed for one night, then two nights—the beginning of two years. I didn't gamble until a fellow came to the motel from Los Angeles to get a divorce—and he introduced me to the crap tables. That was the beginning of every-day gambling. I had my hundred-dollar-a-night budget. Every morning I went to the bank. I either deposited my winnings, or if I had lost the night before, I withdrew my gambling allowance of $100."

The Towne & Country Motel was a sort of classic 1960s moderne, including the extra "e." With an abstract, Mondrian-style, aqua-and-orange-paneled exterior; chevron-shaped signage, flashing "Free TV"; and a turquoise pool with equally turquoise patio umbrellas, its kitsch matched the pervasive kitsch of Las Vegas, then an outpost of the calmer 1950s. An oasis in the high desert of the American southwest, Las Vegas was far removed from the 1960s turmoil. To John, then twenty-six, it seemed a good place to figure out what he wanted to do with his life.

The cultural revolution sweeping the USA didn't appeal to him. Hippies, mind-altering drugs, and psychedelic rock 'n' roll didn't fit into his conservative Germanic perspective. However, there was the craps table.

"I went to Las Vegas for the same reason I came to Canada and the same reason I went to North Bay, Ontario. I am always driven, working long hours, and giving my all. The same was true when I gambled—it satisfied the restless, excitement-seeking part of me, and Las Vegas was exciting. However—two years was too long to indulge. After a while, the Towne & Country Motel only charged me sixty dollars per month because I was a regular. They changed the linen once a week and gave me free gambling tickets because there was no gambling at the motel. The casinos gave those free tickets to motels to lure their customers into the casinos."

The rules governing play at the craps table are complex, but among the various types of gambling in Las Vegas, like blackjack, it gives a disciplined player the best chances. The odds of winning and/or losing are almost 50/50.

Says John about odd experiences at the casinos, "I found it interesting, even eerie. I would stand before the crap table with that negative, losing feeling, put down my bet and lose. When I had that positive, winning feeling, I'd win. However, there were always hesitations; I never totally trusted that intuition. So, I didn't double the bets, when I should have, or didn't place any bets when I felt that negative feeling. Weird. Running a business is much like gambling. One takes calculated risks. It is exciting, and when it works out, it is exhilarating."

During that period there were nights, after an intense evening of gambling, when he would wake up mumbling, "Seven! Seven!" It made him realize he had to keep the excitement of gambling from becoming an obsession. "I have seen too many gambling 'bums' who lost everything. The casinos used to advertise that they would cash paychecks. Too many paychecks were cashed, and too many workers went home broke. Without question, gambling is like any other addiction. I had to stop."

John always kept to his budget. Except once. He'd already lost his gambling budget for the day. He was left with only the money earmarked to get his car out of the repair shop. Temptation was calling. He lost that money too. So, he asked a friend to lend him the money, promising to pay him back the next day.

"He gave me the cash. And guess what? I was a gambler, and what do gamblers do? I went back to the craps table determined to win my losses back. Determination yes, but I lost it all again. That was a wake-up call. I waited for the next day for the bank to open and cleared up the money I owed."

This anxiety over indebtedness, he explains, has extended from his hardscrabble childhood in East Germany to the present day. He hates paying interest, and he never does on his private account. Frugality, he believes, is the path to serenity, even success. Of course, with business it is a different story: "I borrowed as much money from the banks as I could. You could say I built my business with the bank's money." He continues:

> While my evenings were filled with socializing or gambling, there was too much idle time during the day, so I took a job at Western Foods, selling bulk meat around Las Vegas, on commission. It was something I knew a lot about, having done it with Domestic Foods during my time in North Bay. The owner of Western Foods lived in a beautiful house, with two pretty daughters. One day, I was invited to their home for dinner. They sat down to the meal, and as I recall, my boss's wife said, "You seem like a nice young man. Do you mind if, after dinner, we tell you about something that's important to us?"
>
> Well, I wanted to eat, so I agreed and thought, *What are they going to talk me into? Fuller Brush, Amway, or some other scheme?*
>
> However, that evening was the beginning of a new chapter in my life. My hosts introduced me to their Christian beliefs and answered questions that made sense. For instance, that many experiences in this life are like an embryo of things to come, or that our performances or actions of this life reach into eternity, or mankind's eternal progression, and much more . . . it was all inspiring to me. I had never believed in the general Christian idea of Heaven and Hell. Is it fair that one person goes to Heaven and the next person tells a little lie more than the first person and goes to Hell? For eternity? If there is a loving God, he would never let that happen. In my youth

I had been taught that God was more of a policeman, watching and saying, "John Volken, I see what you are doing—quit that," as he gives me a "ticket." Now I see him as my eternal Heavenly Father, who loves me.

I accepted these teachings, and with time, these wonderful ideas brought about a profound change in my life. It didn't take long before I got baptized and became a member of The Church of Jesus Christ of Latter-day Saints. It was the beginning of an ongoing journey. I grew up as a Lutheran and always enjoyed going to church. But I didn't have the studious religious interest some others had. So, after being baptized, it was a rocky road at first, but change came gradually . . . very gradually. I don't know exactly when I said, "Okay, I am in." But with that change, my life became more meaningful.

Once I joined the Church, my social life really took off. It seemed that their youth program, from eighteen to thirty (I was twenty-six) had activities every day. I also quit gambling and acquired a job managing a large department that included the camera section of a local department store. I admit I knew little about cameras. My younger brother Roger had followed me to Las Vegas, just as he'd followed me from East Germany to West Germany in the 1950s, and as he followed me from West Germany to Canada in early 1960. I arranged for a job for him in the camera section of another Las Vegas store. Roger knew all about cameras. Cameras were his life. At one time I phoned him saying, "Roger, I've got a camera here. It's a Nikon. A customer wants me to take out the film. How do I do that?"

As Roger explains, "My brother John was the manager. He didn't want to ask an employee and admit that he, as the manager, didn't know his business and couldn't do a simple task like taking out the 35-mm film—so, I gave him the step-by-step lesson on how to do that. I wouldn't dare apply for a job in a department store if I didn't know anything about a major part of the business—in this case, cameras. But John . . . that never kept him from doing stuff. He thinks about things and decides whether he can or can't do it. If he decides he can do it, he ends up doing it, and doing it well. It points to his confidence and his people skills—the way people like him. He's an extremely sociable guy."

John's stack of photo albums is testimony to his sociability, including the album that contains pictures from his time in Las Vegas. There's the Towne & Country Motel with his blue Beetle parked in front of the door of his ground-level room, and there's the Golden Nugget, and there's the Grand Canyon, and a lot of photos of his many friends sitting beside the motel's swimming pool, or laughing while at a party, or posing amid the red-rock badlands that surround Las Vegas. In the dozens of photos, John's hair grows longer—almost down to his shoulders. That was the trend in the late 1960s.

Says John as he scans the photo album's pages, "Las Vegas was a time of aimlessness and irresponsibility. The summers are hot. I spent a lot of time at the pool or lake, or on day trips to the Grand Canyon, or watching my share of those famous Las Vegas shows. During those two years in Las Vegas, I didn't really accomplish anything. Looking back at that time period, perhaps I have learned the value of time. Once I joined the LDS Church, more than ever, I realized I had to do something worthwhile with my life. I was pushing thirty. Well, twenty-seven or twenty-eight. You know that age? You think you'll live forever. With my newfound beliefs, I found a purpose."

His route west along Highway 80 in 1967 had originally been aimed at Mexico and romance, but John's aimlessness and Las Vegas's many temptations had intervened. Sometimes, he admits now, he thought of Maria during those Las Vegas years. She was pretty and enticing. With a smile, he jokes that he wonders if she's still waiting. However, he's glad he didn't go to Mexico. "If I'd gone, I wouldn't have joined the Church, and my life would have possibly taken a different course."

During his last few months in Las Vegas, John began to realize that total freedom, indulgences, doing whatever one wants to do, when one wants to do it, is—in his words—"not what it is cracked up to be. Freedom without purpose is a waste." So, the time for being a casual playboy, hanging out at the pool, partying, and gambling came to an end.

"Free and purposeless reaps a shallow reward," John observes. "Some people, born with a 'silver spoon' never accomplish much. How boring! I believe it is important to experience hardship and to learn how to handle it. It will make us stronger. I experienced it many times in my life and began to realize life's purpose—namely to prepare to meet our Maker."

In the back of his mind during those transient years, John knew that in almost a decade of wandering he'd likely end up in Vancouver. He'd heard a lot about the place. People in Eastern Canada say they dream about moving to that city one day. The beauty. The mountains. The rivers. The valleys. The forest. The climate. "So, Vancouver was always on my mind."

Therefore, in July 1968, he packed his car and headed north to Vancouver, Canada. It would be there, he assured himself, that his wandering would stop.

In this, he was almost wrong.

At the northbound Blaine customs post on the Washington/British Columbia border, the Canadian official noted John's name, his immigration status, and his two-year-old Quebec license plate and told him, "You've been two years out of the country. And you're German—with a visa to be in Canada. You can't just leave Canada for two years and then get back in. You can't come back to Canada."

A little annoyed, John said, "Where do you want me to go?"

The official calmly replied, "Go back where you came from."

John turned around, and at the American side told the officer that the Canadians wouldn't let him in, to which the man replied, "You were illegally in this country. We can't let you back in."

So, John turned around again and told the Canadian official, "They won't let me back in."

The Canadian immigration officer replied without emotion, "Then you'll have to go back to Germany and reapply for an immigration visa for Canada."

That came as a shock. *Oh no! This isn't good—in fact, this is very bad,* John thought.

He was stuck in "no man's land" at Peace Arch Park, caught in an international bureaucratic snafu. "That I was concerned was an understatement! Back to Germany!? That was easier for them to say than for me to do. Panic!"

The official said, "You've broken the law—you have been staying outside Canada for two years as a foreigner."

As John remembers:

I sat there for hours on the bench. Every so often I checked in at the counter and asked about their plans for me, to which they replied, "We don't know. You can't come into Canada."

After many hours of my very anxious waiting, an official I'd never seen before waved at me and said, "So, tell me about yourself."

I was very humble and said, "Well, I didn't know the law about leaving Canada and not coming back in. I was on vacation."

He asked, "What do you want to do?"

Very emphatically, I replied, "I want to go back into Canada. I love Canada."

"Really?"

"Yes," I confirmed, "I want to be a Canadian."

And after this short conversation, he looked at me compassionately and said, "Okay. Go ahead."

That was one of those moments where I thought, *Thank you! Thank you! Thank you!"*

CHAPTER 5

THE MAVERICK BUSINESSMAN
Pushing Limits, Making Money, and Having Fun

John hadn't lied to the Immigration official at the Canadian border in 1968. He wanted to become a Canadian citizen and make Canada his home. He was confident about his future. From a young age, he had demonstrated entrepreneurship and was always committed to a cause.

In Ontario, he had left Markham Florist for North Bay against the petition of his boss, who wanted him to stay because he valued him as a worker. He told John he'd always be welcomed back.

In North Bay, where he had been washing dishes for twenty-five cents per hour and all he could eat (he loves Chinese food), his boss, a Chinese Christian, took a liking to him and presented him with a pocket-size Bible.

Working hard came easily to John. He liked making things happen and didn't mind the eighteen-hour days when he renovated and sold houses.

Yet, once he left the USA to go back to Canada, he had the intention of being a more responsible, church-going, sober-minded member of The Church of Jesus Christ of Latter-day Saints. Socially and politically, he was—and still is—conservative by nature. But he was—and still is—rebellious against regulations that he feels interfere with his right to be different, industrious, and successful. Restrictive rules were, to his mind, meant to be questioned and sometimes bent. Having been baptized in his newfound faith while in Las Vegas, he accepted what was viewed as the proper conduct for a good citizen and a good Christian, but he didn't always abide by a strict interpretation of these rules. He was twenty-seven when he arrived in Vancouver, and like many young men, took a *laissez-faire* approach to spiritual obligations.

He says of that footloose, late 1960s time, "The Church provided a community, guidance, and a place to socialize. It felt right and good. With time, it became more and more a part of my life's compass, and today, the gospel inspires me to continually try to become a better person."

But the Vancouver that John arrived in was not the Vancouver it became. Across North America, in fact, the values and attitudes that prevailed during the post-war decades between 1945 and 1965 were being challenged. Social, political, and cultural institutions were being questioned. In Vancouver in 1969, anti-war activists were organizing to stop a series of atomic bomb tests on a remote Alaskan island. This group became Greenpeace, the world's largest environmental organization. A group of nudists organized a "Nude-In" that year below the ocean-side University of British Columbia campus. It became Wreck Beach, North America's most popular clothing-optional beach. A neighborhood Chamber of Commerce began warning parents about "hippie free-love practices." Sunday services at the University Hill United Church were promoted by having rock music and go-go dancers. Protests, demonstrations, and marijuana busts featured regularly in local news.

But none of this youthful rebellion—the legendary drugs, sex, and rock 'n' roll—affected John once he'd arrived in Vancouver. Marijuana didn't interest him. He began to realize that he had no time for liberal thinking, and he developed a more and more conservative attitude. He feels growing up in communist East Germany played a large part in why to this day Ronald Reagan is one of his heroes.

For now, he settled in downtown Vancouver's West End, a residential district where rooming houses were rapidly being replaced by high-rise towers. It was, he quickly discovered, a good place for a young bachelor—with a nearby beach on English Bay, a vibrant urban life on Denman and Davie streets, and plenty of opportunities to socialize and date.

It took no time at all for him to find a job. With his experience in North Bay selling freezers filled with pre-packaged meats and frozen foods, he found in the Yellow Pages a freezer food company doing precisely what he'd been doing successfully in Ontario.

He describes what happened next: "On the phone, I told the owner of the meat company that I'd done this work before, and I offered to sell for them. The man said, 'Oh, don't bother. We are going out of business.'"

After a short conversation, though, they agreed to talk and maybe sort out business possibilities. So, in typical John fashion, when given bad news, he took the opportunity to find a positive outcome to the situation. At a subsequent face-to-face meeting, John learned that the freezer food company, instead of paying the meat company, had used the money to start a boat and trailer company, which went bankrupt, leaving the meat company "holding the bag." John saw an opportunity and helped to get them back on their feet. They agreed on certain terms. When John got involved, the company became successful again and everyone celebrated. But within a short time, his boss began to grumble that John was making more money than he did. As a result, John quit and started his own freezer-food business.

He rented an office, hired a team of salespeople, made arrangements with Steveston Meat in nearby Richmond, BC, to supply the frozen food, and in no time, business was booming. He named his company Burmount Foods.

An article in the *Vancouver Province*, dated November 8, 1971, explains in laudatory terms—typical of newspaper business pages—how Burmount worked: Customers would receive a list of scores of available frozen products from which they could select specific cuts of beef and pork, plus frozen fish, chicken, luncheon meats, fruit juices, fruits, and vegetables. At $500 for the Basic Burmount Order, John's promotional material suggested this was enough to provide typical customers with about fifty percent of their half-year supply of frozen food. No freezer— no problem. Burmount Foods would supply one. The pitch that John used in advertising his business was that customers benefited by buying bulk. This was made possible by cutting out the middleman in getting their frozen food directly from the wholesaler. They would receive free delivery and be supplied with a line of credit, if necessary, through the different finance companies.

The larger the food order, the more profit to the business. The food orders were funded by finance companies. The interest was high, which was included in the six-months payment by the customers. John dealt with a branch of the Canadian Imperial Bank of Commerce (CIBC) led by a very aggressive branch manager, who suggested he use the CIBC to have the food orders financed. With low bank interest, John could sell one-year food orders, and the payments were still lower than being subsidized by finance companies. But one-year orders, between $1,000 and $1,800 could not fit in a freezer, so the orders were delivered in two parts—the customer would simply phone Burmount when they could accept the second part of the order. The finance companies verified every delivery, which could take up to three months after the sale. The bank would deposit the proceeds from the food order contract in Burmount's account immediately after the customer's credit was approved. The CIBC would then receive the amount owing from Burmount's customers in monthly installments. This meant money-in-hand for John, since the CIBC would pay him the customer's full payment before Burmount delivered the second portion of goods. It was a cash-flow dream as the company's bank account swelled. The newspaper article reported that in eighteen months, Burmount had grown from a small, one-man, Vancouver office to sales offices across BC, with over 4,000 customers. And John had plans to expand into Alberta, Saskatchewan, and Manitoba.

"I hate having money in the bank," he says. "Money's meant to be used."

So, with Burmount's extraordinary cash flow and his fierce entrepreneurial energy fueled by financial success, John bought a five-acre blueberry farm in Richmond, BC and took over Steveston Meats, an established meat-packing plant that supplied Burmount with their orders. He then opened seven Metro Vancouver clothing stores called Threadsetters and purchased land on Vancouver's Southeast Marine Drive to build a mini-mall, which would, in time, provide space for his planned, relocated meat-packing plant from Richmond as well as a rental space.

These responsibilities meant long, late-night hours running his expanding business and little time for social and cultural life. But he was used to that. It was his life. He sometimes slept in his office, as there was not enough time to drive home. He did the books, hired the staff, oversaw the various business operations, designed the advertising, and dealt with lawyers and wholesale suppliers and customers. He was wary of creating a traditional corporate hierarchy of vice-presidents and department heads, preferring to do things himself. In these ways, he learned a lot. Delegation, he admits now, was not his strongest suit. Work was, in fact, almost everything: his pleasure, his aggravation, his machinations, and his profits.

"I always was a rebel. I listened to advice, yes, but then did it my way," John says, as he reflects on the origins of his early years of learning and earning. "I didn't think about a particular career. I was too busy building the business and making money every day except Sundays." His belief system was paramount.

He bought a one-bedroom condominium in one of North Vancouver's six Woodcroft towers, adjacent to the Capilano River and the Park Royal Shopping Centre. From his ninth-floor balcony, he could look south over Lions Gate Bridge and Stanley Park to the ever-growing number of high-rise buildings appearing in downtown Vancouver. At one of the three Woodcroft swimming pools, he swam laps every morning before going to work. He loved that place: the walks along the forested riverbank, the ease of shopping nearby, the views over Burrard Inlet and English Bay. And every second year he bought a new Corvette.

John lived his entrepreneurial dream until he decided to expand his Burmount Food Processors business into Alberta. But it would not turn out as expected. In BC, John had had an arrangement with the CIBC, in which he signed the Burmount contracts with his customers, and the bank would extend credit to—and receive payments from—these people based on the contracts signed by John. When he tried to establish the same protocol in Calgary, Alberta, he was informed by the CIBC management there, "We can't do that. What the bank is doing in Vancouver is illegal. Consumer contracts have to be signed at the bank, by a bank officer, not at a customer's residence by commissioned salespeople."

That was not what John wanted to hear. "I remember being a little bit cocky when I replied, 'Of course, we can do that. We've been doing it for a long time in BC.'"

Well, John didn't win the battle, and he most certainly lost that war. Pretty soon there were financial inspectors from the bank's head office in Toronto talking to John, telling him in no uncertain terms that his business arrangement in Vancouver was incorrect and that the CIBC headquarters in Toronto was now insisting the bank quit financing John's food orders.

"I made it clear to them," says John, recalling the battle with the bank, "if you discontinue financing us, we'll be out of business within three months. That timespan is our financial cushion. We count on the cash flow. We can't continue to deliver the second half of the food orders, and our customers—which are your customers now—won't make the payment." Visiting bank officials went back to Toronto's head office with the news: "We are stuck. If we discontinue financing Burmount Food, they won't be able to deliver the second portion of their food orders, and they'll go out of business. We'll then have to cope with very negative consequences." Since the contracts, as everyone by then agreed, were illegal, the bank would end up with more than just a "black eye."

Months passed, and the legal wrangling went on and on. There were meetings, lawyers, consumer loans officers, accountants, offers, and counter-offers. The vice-president for Consumer Loans from Toronto showed up trying to play it down by saying he'd stopped by from a trip to Japan. The fact was that the CIBC was trying feverishly to make the best out of a bad situation. John argued that he had bought Steveston Meats with twenty meat cutters employed there. He had seven Threadsetter stores—with multi-year leases. He had bought a blueberry farm. He had a major investment in a mini mall under construction on Southeast Marine Drive. And he had 8,000 Burmount customers who had loans to pay off to the CIBC for the credit line they'd been granted.

The CIBC promised John that if he liquidated these acquired assets, they'd provide a financial arrangement for the survival of his Burmount business and the meatpacking plant.

John did all that was requested. He sold the blueberry farm at a profit and sold the construction site for a profit as well. He even closed the seven Threadsetter stores at a significant loss because he had to buy out the multi-year leases for which he had contractual obligations to pay.

He did all that based on the CIBC's promise that it would grant a bridge loan to re-establish Burmount's business under a new financing arrangement with a finance company. This commitment was witnessed in front of Burmount lawyers and CIBC lawyers and their vice-president of Consumer Loans. Burmount Foods was always profitable, but they needed at least a year to switch from one-year food orders financed by the bank to six-month orders financed by the finance company. At the same time, they would deliver the second portion of the one-year order.

When the time came for the bank to make good on their promise, there was no reply.

John headed to Toronto to see the man in charge, the vice-president of Consumer Loans. This was the very man who had made the promise in Vancouver in front of all the witnesses. John arrived at the Toronto CIBC's head office only to learn that the man was not even prepared to see him. He learned that the offer of a bridge loan was, in fact, a lie. The goal had been to induce John to re-capitalize his Burmount investment by selling his other businesses and using the money to deliver the second portions of the food contracts. John admits, "I was too naïve in believing bank officials to be trustworthy. Lesson learned."

Back in Vancouver, John told his lawyer, "I want to have my day in court. There were witnesses to their promise of a bridge loan. About ten people witnessed the negotiation: lawyers, accountants, bank officials, my general manager, my brother Roger, and me. We all witnessed the promise."

The lawyer explained, "John, you won't find any credible law firm that'll defend the case. They all depend on banks for business—negotiating contracts, dealing with mortgages, loans, investments."

Of the CIBC, John says, "They screwed us. We did everything they asked us to do and more. They promised a bridge loan. They lied! Lesson learned: You can't trust a guy just because he's a bank vice-president, or a minister of a church, or this or that. It was very disappointing. I cut up my CIBC credit cards. Maybe all banks would deal that way to protect themselves—even if they must lie, but I never again set foot in the CIBC. They fired the bank manager who extended the loan arrangement for the Burmount food orders."

Looking back, John says he should not have liquidated the assets, which would have forced the bank to work with him. It could have prevented this very agitating situation in which he found himself.

> We continued to deliver the second half of the food orders until the money ran out. It was on a Saturday night that the management team got together. It seemed to be the end of the road. Or was it?
>
> I remembered the time the Lalji family wanted to buy Burmount Foods when it was a thriving business. But now? I called them and they came into the Burmount office the next day. The father was with his three sons.
>
> The father, who was without question the patriarch, said nothing the entire time, just listened and nodded or shook his head as the sons negotiated the buying of Burmount. We talked mostly about the operation of the business. I was up against the wall. One thing I knew was certain—if they put enough money into the business to finance the second half of the food orders, they had a profitable business. They agreed.
>
> Unfortunately, I had no idea what price tag I should put on the company. They offered me "peanuts"—I took it. I gave every employee $5,000, the bank was off the hook, and Burmount survived.

John had lost a profitable and fun business. He was down but not out. He licked his wounds . . . but was soon back on his feet. As he says today of those times when business efforts collide with realities, "When something doesn't work out, I don't dwell on it. I learn from it and move on. Overcoming adversity builds character and prepares one for the next challenge. So, what's next?"

Being done with the frozen food business, John's relentless drive and energy led him to go into the mail-order business. He was always intrigued by businesses that looked like they were a good bet to grow. Mail order was one of those. The exciting thing is that one has the whole world as a customer base. In North Bay, Ontario, he dabbled in the mail order business on a small basis. It was fun. Mimicking the popular, 1961 self-help guide he'd read a decade before, Napoleon Hill's *Think & Grow Rich*, John began collecting ideas from newspaper lifestyle clippings, *Popular Mechanics* blurbs, trendy business articles, promotional business pitches, and conversations with friends. He was especially drawn to ideas that might be pursued by those looking for a home business or second income, and he gathered over 700 suggestions about ways to earn money at home, part-time.

He wrote a book and settled on the title, *1002 Incredible Ways to Make Money*. A banner on the cover read: BECOME INDEPENDENT—START WITHOUT MONEY!

It proved to be a one-off publishing experiment. He sold about 6,000 copies, all through the mail.

At that time, his Burmount Foods ex-sales manager wanted to start a freezer food company but couldn't get a finance company to finance his food orders. He approached John to be his partner. John wouldn't have to do any work, simply lend his name to the business, which was all that was needed to get the financing. John agreed, but before long, he got involved on a full-time basis. His brother Roger was working as a store manager in a photo retail store. Roger had a family by now and was barely making ends meet. John offered him half of his share in the new business—which would give him a quarter of the business. But then John's half-partner suggested dividing the shares three ways. John found that very generous of his partner—he didn't have to do that.

John sold his mail-order business and was back to selling bulk freezer-food orders. Now there were three of them, all making serious money. Only this time, his customers would pay and purchase six-month instead of twelve-month orders, and it would be financed by a finance company, not a bank. He called this latest incarnation Westland Food Packers.

In a 1978 brochure illustrating the company's operation, three dates—1905, 1950, and NOW—are accompanied by drawings of an old-fashioned general store (1905), a supermarket (1950), and a truck parked at a Westland warehouse (NOW). The promotional copy read: "Cut out the middleman. Save money." Franchise opportunities were also sold for $14,200.

Through franchising, Westland's operation rapidly spread across Western Canada. John had Westland warehouses and meat packers and hundreds of salesmen working on straight commissions in Calgary, Edmonton, Regina, and Winnipeg. And the three partners found their bank accounts once again filling with money from licensing and profits from bulk-food-order sales.

During his years in direct sales, John had observed the eccentric qualities of an average commissioned salesperson. They often don't like structure and tend to come and go at will. "Some applied for the work," says John, "looking like a million dollars, but they were useless as salespeople. Others looked like farm boys, and I hesitated to give them a sales kit or spend time training them. But—surprise—they came in with the signed contracts."

Reflecting on those times, John says, "Commissioned salespeople, as a whole, are very independent. They don't like regular hours or any other kind of restrictions. Some are restless, always pushing, and some are lazy and useless. A good commissioned salesperson should always be 'hungry.' I can relate to them—I was one of them. Whatever I did, I always pushed the limit. I was this come-and-go guy in the 1960s and 1970s in Las Vegas and Vancouver, and so were my commissioned salespeople. It was fun and rewarding. Our Christmas parties were festivities to be remembered. Everything was free, except for the booze. You wanted to drink—you had to pay. They didn't mind. The parties were a riot."

This realization about understanding and managing people would prove useful twenty years later when John first became involved with Vancouver's homeless, marginalized, addicted street people. *Everyone has a song to sing,* he told himself. *Sometimes it is well hidden, but we must never judge a book by its cover.*

As the late 1970s passed and Westland Food carried on, John faced several personal and career issues that redirected his life. He was approaching forty. He'd experienced the world of business, learned about human behavior, had a beautiful condo, drove a Corvette, had money in the bank, had an active social life, and was having a lot of fun. But to what end?

John says about this gradual change of attitude toward life's purpose: "Making money came easy. But little by little, making easy money lost its challenge, and I realized that making money never really was the reason for me to do business. It was more the challenge. The business life can be exciting—it was for me. And selling bulk food orders didn't have the future I wanted. Besides, the government put more and more restrictions on that type of direct sales. I wanted to create a business that benefitted the consumer. There were also both practical and, I realized, ethical reasons. I needed a new direction—time for a change."

An eighteen-year-long career in direct-marketing frozen foods was done. "That was the end of it," John simply says.

It was March 1981. Directly across East Hasting Street from his office, John saw a "For Rent" sign in the window of a vacant store. He'd already begun to hatch a scheme for a new business, something that could be big, global, and—if he were right—make millions. It would be based on sound ethical and economic priorities.

As he crossed the street to get the phone number on the sign, he didn't know where that moment would lead. An empty store. An odd idea. Crossing the street that day was pivotal to all that has happened for him between then and now.

CHAPTER 6

GO BIG OR GO HOME
An Empire Is Built by Taking Risks

John had been thinking about how people sell houses. There was the seller, the buyer, and the realtor. This allowed people in one town to buy a property available in another town. *What if,* he thought, *I do the same thing with furniture, equipment, artwork, cars, machines, even airplanes . . . anything an owner wants to sell.* Perhaps someone in New York had a Cessna for sale—the plane someone in Oklahoma was looking for. Get seller and buyer together, and the company makes a small commission on each transaction. The potential was huge. He envisioned a location in every town. It could be operated out of a kitchen. The world would be his marketplace. Go big or go home. The idea was exciting, and he was set to start his new venture. He called it United Buy & Sell Service (UB&S).

From the perspective of the twenty-first century, John has come to realize that what he did in 1981 when he set up his first United Buy & Sell Service store was, essentially, the precursor to a little company called eBay (its 2018 sales were over $37 billion with over $10 billion in profit). He's well aware that in the thirty-seven-year gap between then and now, computers and the Internet have made possible what was impossible in the age of IBM Selectric typewriters and newspaper advertising.

He rented the store on East Hastings in Vancouver for $4,000 a month and put up a big sign: "United Buy & Sell Service". Plastered on the windows, in bold yellow and red, were posters that read "Canada's Super Discount Centre" or "Buy . . . Sell . . . Trade" or "Furniture . . . Household

Goods." It didn't take him long, however, to discover that soliciting consignments in tiny classified ads would not produce the volume and quality of merchandise to fill his store and pay for the overhead. He bought a van, hired an assistant, and quickly began to add to his inventory by attending estate sales and offering to buy everything—lock, stock, and barrel—in order to relieve vendors of their goods.

"I remember friends thought I was crazy," he says. "They knew I drove a Corvette and had a beautiful condo, but making a successful global business out of marketing used merchandise?" That was all the more challenge to John, who was determined to make it work.

At first, he sought listings of estate sales, visited vendors' homes, and ferried his van full of furniture back to the store. Late at night, he'd repair slightly damaged items, polish the wood, and try to remove stains from couches. Then, as his inventory increased and space filled up, he'd stack the big items like sofas and mattresses one on top of another. By Friday, the store would be full, and he'd advertise ridiculously low prices—"Sofas—$99", "Desks—$49", "Mattresses—$50." All used, but in good condition. By closing time on Saturday, the store would often be half-empty. This went on for the first year, when he realized that, with monthly rent, salaries, taxes, the difficulties in searching for the right used merchandise, and other overhead to be paid, the success he had envisioned would be an uphill battle. It didn't help that the location had two fundamental flaws as a retail store. The first was that during rush hours there were "No Stopping" signs out front, and the second was that there were stairs to the elevated back door. Both were serious impediments to receiving and loading furniture.

Faced with these challenges and determined to find a solution, John reached back to his experience of making money through selling frozen-food franchises. He would get other people to work independently for him. He advertised, "Business Opportunities for Men with Trucks," and urged respondents, "Go out and buy estate sales, bring us what you buy, and when it sells, you get half the money." It was brilliant. A win-win situation, and it saved the day.

"At one time, I had six men with trucks or vans hustling furniture. They'd bought it cheap . . . maybe for forty dollars at an estate sale. Sometimes they'd get a whole load for free. We would sell it and make a healthy profit. But there were occasional times when they bought a nice used sofa, say for $200. We would sell it for $300, meaning the buyer got $150 so he lost fifty. They learned fast. They would deliver the sold goods and keep the delivery charges. Most of the time it was a win-win situation and no investment on my part. I made lemonade, for a time, out of lemons."

Within one year, John opened a second store in Surrey and a third in Coquitlam, both cities in Metro Vancouver. Gradually, through the early 1980s, he built his business to six stores, but he realized the idea of a consignment-based service had its limits and wasn't viable enough. He changed the name from United Buy and Sell Service to United Buy and Sell Furniture Warehouse.

"I built my office in the warehouse basement in the main store. There was no insulation in the walls and floor, so when the winter came, it was cold," he recalls. "The only warmth came from a small space heater, which was not enough to keep me warm, but it was okay. During the day, I was busy working the stores, and I did the office work during the evening—payroll, taxes, invoices, correspondence, advertising—the usual. The radio was set to quit playing at midnight to remind me to go home. Often, when the radio started playing again an hour later at 1:00 a.m., it prompted me to go home and get some sleep. I was always back in the office at 7:30 a.m. I was determined."

In fact, throughout his life, working sixty hours a week has been normal for him. And in those early days when his business was growing, it might easily run to eighty-plus hours a week—but never on Sundays.

There were, amid the struggles, a couple of things that changed his direction.

First, he was visited by the owner of a woodworking business who was eager to have UB&S as his customer. It went against John's long-term plan for UB&S to deal only in estate sales and consignment sales. But when he put some new chests on floor display, they sold quickly, as did the second and third batches. *Maybe*, he thought, *selling both new and used furniture might be a way to increase the business, and instead of searching for sellable merchandise, the new furniture would be delivered.*

Secondly, after opening his sixth store, and stocking it with mostly new furniture, he began to see that with each passing month, this store was doing better than the others. This prompted his conclusion that he should change direction, perhaps abandon the Buy & Sell aspect of the business, and commit himself to dealing entirely with new furniture and mattresses.

He shared his intention to switch from consignment sales to new furniture and mattresses with a friend, who at the time managed the largest furniture store in the Vancouver area:

> My friend tried to discourage me by starting out with: "There is a lot of competition in this business—you don't stand a chance."
>
> That didn't discourage me, and I shot back with "I am just as competitive, and there are a few things I'll do differently. For starters, I won't open on Sundays."
>
> My friend's reply was, "John, you're on the wrong track! Saturdays and Sundays are the biggest days for furniture sales. That's when husbands and wives get together to buy their furniture."
>
> I replied with, "Listen there is more. I won't have those exaggerated price-reducing sales, like up to eighty percent off. It's not believable. I'll have everyday low prices."
>
> "No sales?" said my friend. "Why do you think we have those sales? That's when we make money. This bait and switch sale is how the furniture business works."
>
> I continued, "I won't have commissioned salespeople. Letting customers know the salesperson is on salary puts them at ease."
>
> My friend emphatically answered with, "That is wishful thinking. Furniture is sold by commissioned salespeople. I am your friend and have been in the business all my life. Save your money."

Salespeople are motivated by commission. John knew that. His previous businesses all had commissioned salespeople, so he was well aware of the advantages. Against the advice of virtually every person working in retail furniture sales, and the advice of many working for him, John ran his growing business with several perplexing and counterintuitive principles. United Furniture Warehouse never opened on Sunday, never had a sale, and their salespeople were on a salary—not commission. John ended up with 150 stores, and ended up renting the store where his friend used to work because its owner had discontinued the business. Again and again, his experiences with "experts" were confirmed: Don't trust the often-self-anointed experts.

John came to create his own list of the qualities necessary for success as a (retail) salesperson. Here are only a few:

- Use appropriate language or phrases. When you first meet a customer don't say, "Can I help you?" They'll probably reply, "No." Rather greet him with a friendly: "What are you looking for today?" To that they cannot say, "No." They may say, "Oh, I'm just looking." You then reply with, "Oh, what in particular are you looking for?"

- People buy from people they like. Turn possible negatives into positives—get involved—be passionate—emotional—show that you care.

- Create a need—benefit. Make people feel that they want to buy, not that they are being sold.

- A professional salesperson knows when to listen and when to talk. You must know a potential buyer's wishes and objections.

- It's not important what you like. If people want a pink mattress to go with their pink curtains, you create a reason(s) to support that wish, even if you think it is crazy.

"If you know how to sell, you're never out of a job," says John. "It doesn't matter whether it is a pen or a car, a broom or a piece of furniture. If you know how to sell, there are always plenty of jobs to choose from." In the past, this skill set had given John considerable confidence.

Following the opening of his Nanaimo store in the mid-1980s, John rode a wave of changing interior design values, and economic confidence, toward his late-1980s financial success. He kept the name, United Buy & Sell Furniture

Warehouse. "If it ain't broke don't fix it." However, he gradually shifted the stores' emphasis from used to new, lower-end furniture, and with time he upgraded the quality. But with stocking the stores with inventory, warehousing, fixturing each store, and paying taxes, there was never enough money. "We always pushed for increases in the line of credit from the bank, and they worked with us. Then, from the time we opened the sixth store, we had more money for our advertising budget, and we never looked back," John says. "We were excited about having a positive cash flow. So, we opened a seventh store. And then an eighth. Every store was successful. Once we had opened the eighth or ninth store, we enjoyed an even faster increase and growth. We had a full-time realtor travelling and scouting for new locations. Business was good, exciting, and profitable."

As previously mentioned, John changed his name in 1977 from Volker Jahn to John Volken, which was another of his personality characteristics: "Keep it simple, stupid." Roger Jahn, John's younger brother and associate for a time, reflected on how John turned the struggling company into the success it became. "John is patient. He makes a plan. He convinces himself of its potential. He works on it. He wouldn't have achieved his success without his extreme determination and stick-to-it-ness."

In retrospect, the success of his furniture business was a fairly straight path. There were a couple of stages where he changed when it was appropriate to change. "In business one has to be flexible," says John and he is, even though some people call him stubborn . . . which he can also be. He started expanding when furniture moved from being an investment into being a fashion item. In the past, people had bought furniture as a lifetime purchase. Then in the mid-1980s, people started changing their interiors—buying new stuff, getting rid of the old, and passing it on to their kids. John had not thought about it in such terms when he started shifting his business paradigm to selling new furniture, but that's how it evolved. Luck certainly had something to do with it. Roger said, "You cannot attribute John's success entirely to luck though. He is talented."

During this period of early struggle and ultimate growth, luck played an almost comic part in his business. One day a man named James Griffin came into John's East Hastings street office trying to sell John on the idea that his business needed an advertising jingle. John's response was, "Yeah, right. A jingle? I don't need a jingle. I need to sell a sofa so I can pay the rent for the next month."

The guy begged to differ: "You do need a jingle. I'll sell you one for $900. It's a bargain. And I'll do better than that: if you don't like it, you don't have to pay for it."

"Fine," John agreed. He wanted to get rid of him and decided right then he wouldn't like the jingle.

"About a month later," John relates, laughing at the memory, "James Griffin reappears in my office."

"Remember me, the guy with the jingle?"

He played the jingle on his tape recorder:

Who's got the latest style around?
Who's got the lowest price in town?
Who makes the competition nervous?
United Buy and Sell Service. Boom, Boom!

> I wasn't moved by what I heard and remembered his promise, "you don't have to pay for it if you don't like it," so I told him "I don't like it."
>
> My attitude about his work obviously offended him. He started to argue with me, "What do you mean you don't like it? It's awesome!"
>
> I thought arguing with a customer wasn't professional. So I simply pointed out why I didn't like it.
>
> He mumbled something like, "Some people think they always know better . . . " and walked out the door and I figured I'd never see him again.
>
> A month later, to my surprise, he returned to tell me that he'd listened to my suggestions, and changed the jingle. And I thought, *Oh, now I'm in trouble.* He expects to get paid. I listened to the tape and yes, it was much better. I paid him the $900 for the jingle and tossed the tape in the drawer and forgot all about it.
>
> (By the way shortly after that, James Griffin went on to start the Vancouver Film School which has become a very successful and prestigious school in Canada and other

parts of the world. I think I might take some credit for
his career change.)

But by then, John had opened several more stores at an ever-increasing rate. He recalls, "One day, when this TV salesman came in and proposed, 'You need to advertise on TV. It will help potential customers to become your customers.' His sales pitch made sense. I was excited, thinking it might be the much-needed answer to our marketing challenge. "But, how do we make an effective TV commercial? Why not smash a panel of glass? That would get people's attention, and then start the commercial. Maybe not. Then I remembered the jingle, 'Wait a minute. I've got this jingle,' I pulled it out of my drawer and played the tape, which ended *United Buy & Sell Service . . . boom, boom!*"

"We made the commercial about furniture, mattresses, and low prices with only the last line of the jingle. It was a hit," John explains. "The very next day after the commercial aired, business went through the roof. It got aired on TV over the next few years many thousands of times. Everyone knew about us because of the catchy jingle—with the boom-boom ending."

Elton Media handled most of United's advertising. Jon Elton has known John Volken for over thirty-five years and remembers well working with John during the "heady" expansion of United Furniture Warehouse. Here is Jon Elton's story:

> I had worked in the advertising business, particularly Television, for many years. When John hired my ad agency in 1983, he had three stores, but was already talking about hundreds of stores, with regional managers over-seeing supervisors over-seeing store managers. John always thought big, and I think he surprised everyone except himself when he accomplished those lofty dreams, along the way taking his ad budget from $200,000 to over $12 million per year. A good client to have. John picked a centrally located city, opened a store, advertised on TV, and its signal covered surrounding cities. Then, when he opened stores in those surrounding cities,

all he needed to advertise was, 'Now open in (city)'. It astounded the competition with how quickly United Furniture could open new locations and be successful. It was almost unfair to our smaller competitors.

John seemed to instinctively know the importance of 'Brand.' When things got really good, or really bad, which happens often in the life of companies, many of them would look to increase short-term profits by cutting money from the ad budget. Not John. He always spent close to 10% of gross sales on advertising. It was almost as sacred to him as not opening on Sundays! He knew investing in the brand was critical to building the size of company he had in mind; he didn't go for short-term gain and it worked! When my agency would try and get too creative, John always brought us back to the basics. What's another way of saying, 'No Frills, No Gimmicks! Low Prices!! Boom Boom?' John was a master marketer! It was a pleasure helping him build his dream!

As the number of his stores continued to increase, and plans for expansion to new store locations across Canada and the United States grew, John needed more qualified help. This growth led John to bring in a young assistant named David Gerstner, a frustrated accountant who would, in time, assume the position of general manager, with his main role being furniture buyer.

Describing David's role, John says, "In the furniture business, as is true in most business, the buying is as important as the approach to selling. Furniture is very much part of a fashion business. It is crucial to be able to follow the trends, and then negotiate the best prices. David was good at that and together we made a winning team."

They'd go to the semi-annual furniture extravaganza in High Point, North Carolina. One could say it is to furniture retailers what Disneyland is to eight-year-olds. Thousands of buyers descend on the town each year, along with hundreds of wholesale reps—plus myriad media flacks,

interior designers, artisans, fabric suppliers, and stiletto-heeled trendset-
ters whose job is to fuel the frenzy. All major wholesalers and importers
are packed into High Point's business district; outside downtown lies
thirty-acre Furnitureland South, a place that bills itself as the World's
Largest Furniture Store. Whereas John had first bought small volumes
of new furniture and household decor in the early years of UB&S, they
now dealt with American, Taiwanese, and Chinese manufacturers and
bought furniture by the container-load. UB&S became one of the largest
furniture chains in North America with over $200 million in sales volume
a year. "That certainly helps to negotiate the best prices," John adds.

About five years after we opened our first store, we were
in need of a warehouse/distribution center to handle the
ever-increasing container shipments. Also, even though I
will fight bureaucracy forever, more office space was desperately needed. I thought it was time to build our future
warehouse/head office. In search of a suitable piece of
land, I visited a five-acre parcel next to the Trans-Canada
Highway and wondered why the area had not been developed. Was there anything I didn't know? The visibility
for our future United Furniture Warehouse head office
store and warehouse seemed unbeatable. Standing on one
corner of the property I saw the street sign on the other
corner . . . I went to see it and wow! It read "United
Boulevard." Someone wanted to tell me something. I
bought the 7.5 acres on the corner—and subsequently
the construction of a big $5 million warehouse store on
that site changed our fortunes forever. Located beside an
exit off the busiest highway in the area, serviced by an
adjacent rail spur, and with room for the needed parking
lot plus warehouse capacity, that location put us on the
map and added a significant boom-boom to my bottom
line. We were the first store on that stretch of United
Boulevard, which soon developed into the furniture hub

in the Vancouver area. The building is worth today, in 2020, about $28,000,000. It was the single best investment I made in my twenty years in the furniture business. My foundation still owns that building, together with several other buildings, which finance my philanthropic efforts.

It was at this time that John made another decision about his rapidly expanding business. The idea came to him, he vividly recalls, while taking a shower in his Deep Cove home. The more he heard the name United Buy & Sell Furniture Warehouse, the more he became convinced that the name should be changed. If he wanted to develop the company to become a major furniture retailer in the USA and Canada with hundreds of stores, then he felt the business needed a new name. He jumped into action. "Stop making signage with the old name. Stop the advertising. Change the jingle. Register the new name." That was in 1994. From then on it would be United Furniture Warehouse.

And here the jingle story continues:

> When I decided to change the company's name from United Buy & Sell Services to United Furniture Warehouse, Jon Elton, who handled our advertising for years, knocked on the door of the man who'd sung the jingle initially and asked him if he'd record it again, only with our new name. He, in the meantime, had become an accomplished opera singer. He had charged fifty dollars for voicing the original jingle (the jingle creator was a friend of his), and added, "I wouldn't do it again for a million dollars! It drives me crazy every time I hear it on TV. Instead of a fifty-dollar buyout, I should have asked for royalties, I'd have been rich!"

John clearly loves this story, laughing at the multiple ironies. It's apparent from his delight at the effect of the then-famous TV jingle that it was pure advertising gold. He found another singer to voice the jingle with a new name . . . no problem.

In 1995, John learned that he was in the running for the prestigious title of Ernst & Young Pacific Region Entrepreneur of the Year, the top business award in Canada. His biography in *BC Business* magazine reported that despite having no retail experience when he established United Buy & Sell Service in 1981, by 1995 he had set up a no-frills, "everyday low prices" juggernaut. Through aggressive investment, expansion, and advertising, the story continued, John had added about ten new stores each year during the preceding decade. The article contained an enlarged pull-quote from John, in which, when asked what he wanted to be known for in life, he answered, "I did my best."

He recalls standing on the stage at the Vancouver Trade and Convention Centre on September 28 that year amid seven other previously announced winners in categories ranging from High Tech to Manufacturing to Services. Like the others, John had already been designated winner of his "Retail" category and had given a brief speech, which included his rendition of the infamous jingle: "*United Furniture Warehouse . . . boom, boom.*" For the first time since the honor was awarded, an overall winner was chosen. Surveying those standing there on the stage, John thought that some of the other businessmen were better known, more worthy, more likely to win the Pacific Region's overall Entrepreneur of the Year prize. So, when he heard, "The overall winner: John Volken, United Furniture Warehouse," he was not prepared for it. He didn't have a second acceptance speech. For two or three seemingly long seconds he stood at the microphone looking for the right thing to say. "I wish my jingle had a second verse," he told the audience, and they laughed. That was the beginning of a better speech than the one he had previously prepared.

"There were about 1,500 business people in the audience," John remembers. "They were all—well, it was great. And Dr. Joe Segal, CM, OBC, LLD (Hon), a leading British Columbia businessman and philanthropist, came up to me and said, 'John, I want you to know I voted for you.' Segal was my hero in retailing. It meant a lot hearing that. He was also inspiring to me in so many other ways—his family, his humanitarian efforts, his work ethic, his business building, and his down-to-earth personality. I love and admire that man."

Said Segal about John, "Everything's risky in business. Things don't necessarily work out. He started with nothing. He opened his first store . . . then a second . . . then a third. And kept going. Pretty soon he had forty stores and was opening his forty-first. He deserved to be Entrepreneur of the Year."

"That night," John says, "I was too excited to sleep. My mind was racing, contemplating my next step. The challenge was gone; I have played the game and won. I had more money than I ever needed. What else is there to tackle?

It's time to give back.

Once we have sufficiently provided for our family,
it is up to our social conscience, our humanity,
and our love for our fellow men
to share our good fortune with those in need.

John O. Volken

By 2003, United Furniture Warehouse had grown to 151 locations with over $200 million in sales in the USA and Canada. Over the years, the Brick Furniture Warehouse people had approached John about a possible sale of his company—the answer was always, "No." But now, as he was entangled in an acrimonious divorce, things had changed. The result was a quick sale. He donated the proceeds of the sale, together with United's real estate holdings, to charities by creating two foundations: one in the USA and one in Canada. The USA proceeds from the sales were transferred into the USA foundation and the proceeds in Canada into the Canadian Foundation. These foundations now fund the John Volken Academies, Lift the Children orphanages, and other charitable endeavors.

CHAPTER 7

LOVE & MARRIAGE, LOVE & MARRIAGE...
It's About Time!

There was this young, attractive woman named Alison Faulk, the daughter of family friends. Over the years, John had watched her grow from a girl into womanhood. To her, he was a charming, family friend. To him, she was a pretty woman he liked having around. She'd ride her bicycle down to John's office . . . and hang out with him. "I'd watch him on the phone," she says today. "Listening to his conversations, watching him having meetings, and doing deals. I loved what I saw. When he wasn't busy, we'd talk."

At age nineteen, Alison took a summer job at John's United Buy and Sell Service, prior to heading to a three-year nursing program at Vancouver General Hospital (VGH). She and John soon began to date. John recalls picking her up at the VGH nurses' residence one evening during Vancouver's Expo 86 World's Fair and hearing the intercom announcement: "Alison Faulk. Your dad is here to pick you up."

Her dad! That is embarrassing. What will she think?

But the age difference never bothered Alison. "Age was never an issue," she says. "I just saw us as equals." What she found attractive was his interest in reading and learning, his dynamic personality, his playfulness, and his love of family. He, in turn, was drawn to her quiet confidence, her beauty, her athletic ability, and her ethic of hard work.

Three years later, as the time approached for Alison to graduate from nursing school—with a job offer from BC Women's Hospital and Health Centre—forces conspired to bring an end to John's long bachelorhood. Alison would soon begin work at the hospital in the post-partum facility where new mothers learned about breast-feeding and baby care, and nurses kept a close eye on the infants' health.

In the late fall of 1987, John summoned the courage to finalize his plan. As Alison recalls it, he asked, "What are your plans?" And she'd replied she'd rent a place near her new job. To which John replied, "Well, why do that? Let's get married!"

They married in February 1988. Alison was twenty-two and John was forty-six. He was more concerned about the age difference than she was. They moved into John's one-bedroom Woodcraft condominium. He loved that place. He had walled the living room with cedar, and he had a big flower container on his deck, a double garage, and a great view of Stanley Park and Lions Gate Bridge. He went out swimming every morning and could walk along the river to North Shore's largest shopping center. He imagined living there forever.

Alison continued working at Children's Hospital until their first child was born nine months later. Wanting to be a full-time mother, she then quit her job. As much as John loved his riverside North Vancouver place, the realities of a new wife, a baby in its bedside crib, and the ongoing pressures of building his furniture business forced the family to move to a new, three-bedroom, creek-side house on the forested slopes of Mt. Seymour in North Vancouver.

Curiously, it was only then—with the birth of his first child—that John began to miss his own father, who had died in action three months before the end of World War II. Despite having no memory of him, John had learned through relatives about his father's many admirable qualities: handsome, tall, intelligent, and a leader. Though as a youngster, he hadn't missed having a dad . . . "When I became a father, I found myself thinking, *I wonder what my dad would do under these circumstances. How would he deal with parental things?* As if I were seeking his advice. I grew close to my dad then, even though I never knew him."

Just as his company grew, so did John's family. Their son Uve's birth on the 22nd of November, 1988 was followed two years later by the birth of Lisanne, a daughter named after John's mother. And two years after that, a second daughter arrived, named Talia. John would have loved to have a half-dozen more children, but each of Alison's pregnancies was accompanied by almost nine months of debilitating hyperemesis. It was a condition that produced very high blood pressure, nausea, and a premature birth. "I was a pre-natal nurse," says Alison of those times:

> I knew what the risks were. I had my head in the toilet half the time, or on the floor with no energy. It wasn't a healthy scene. Three children were enough. John's role as a doting parent and his role as a hard-working businessman meant conflicting demands on his time—except on Sundays, which were dedicated to church, family, and socializing over dinner with friends.
>
> Every morning John would play with the children. He'd be singing "Yankee-Doodle" or "Peter Rabbit," the children's favorites. He would sit and teach them songs. He was very happy and loving with them. It was a good energy when he was around. "Oh, Daddy, Daddy," they'd say, "give me a piggy-back ride." You know how kids are—before school age: "Let's play."
>
> There was a routine where we'd go for a walk in the morning if John was able to. He'd come with us on those walks. He was just as adventurous as the kids and me. He'd be in the woods jumping, "Let's go." And they'd find things in the woods. He was very hands-on that way. But then—around ten in the morning—it's off to work. And I wouldn't see him until midnight, sometimes as late as 3:00 a.m. He'd phone the kids at six or seven each

evening to say, "Good night." I knew he was building his business. I never complained. That's just the way it was.

On the kitchen bulletin board adjacent to Alison's ocean-side window in White Rock, BC, are photos of the three young children Uve, Lisanne and Talia —buried to their necks in sand in Hawaii or posing in Disneyland— just as they are in John's albums.

By 1993—the global economy was recovering from a late 1980s recession and with United Furniture Warehouse continuing to grow, John began working on what he would call his "dream home." He bought a sloping, 1.2-acre lot with a large older house in prestigious British Properties in West Vancouver. Its views east to west encompassed Burrard Inlet, the Lions Gate Bridge, Stanley Park, downtown Vancouver, the Kitsilano and Point Grey neighborhoods, and English Bay. John paid $800,000 for it in 1993. The sellers had bought the house for $60,000 many years ago. The house had been beautiful then and the mortgage had been paid off long ago. Now with the $800,000 from John, the sellers bought a beautiful new home—for about $700,000, so they had money to spare. This was inspiring to John—it represented the American Dream!

John bulldozed the original house, and he and Alison began working on plans that grew in each new architectural iteration into a huge, nearly 14,000-square-foot, $5.5 million home.

Alison says of the five-year-long construction project: "He put his heart into it. It was his baby. To build a home for generations to come was his dream. But, of course, he involved me in every decision. Like: 'Let's go choose kitchens now.' And we'd drive around with the architect and the builder and consider kitchens. They kind of guided us—like, 'You want to have a bedroom for each child? You need a bathroom for each of them nowadays.' That's how we came to have all the bathrooms we had."

She finds it amusing in hindsight how the project expanded in scope and duration through the years of decisions, alteration, and construction.

"John says of the house that there were thirteen bathrooms. But I cleaned them." She counts meticulously on her fingers. "I think there were just twelve," she says, laughing at the last two words.

John solicited opinions about everything from flooring to entertainment facilities to outdoor play areas, and incorporated many into the evolving architectural plans. In the end, the house had a basement ensuite that could accommodate future grown children and grandchildren, a sewing room for Alison, an elevator, a large indoor pool with a Hawaiian-themed fresco on the wall, a staircase that led from the master bedroom to the pool, and a theatre room. Outdoors the property had a running well with a pond, a large vegetable garden, and children's play structures—including a subterranean cave.

Large trees were all around but from his elevated view, the only house in sight was the home of business magnate and philanthropist Jimmy Pattison, one of Canada's most successful businessmen. In 1997, the Volken family of five moved into their sprawling $5.5 million West Vancouver home. It was their "dream home" and the plan was to live there forever. John had come quite a long way from the orphanage in East Germany.

Amidst ongoing discussions about new store openings with United Furniture Warehouse, buying trips to furniture shows, and choices being made about the new home, John began reflecting aloud about how his past and his future might connect. He talked with Alison about his childhood in East Germany—the privations and the daily struggles—and how he and one of his brothers had spent time in an orphanage, and how he'd enjoyed that year. As Alison recalls, he said, "You know what? I want to start an orphanage." To which, she'd pointed out that, in 1993, there weren't orphanages anymore. But maybe—since he wanted more children—they might consider acquiring some foster kids? This idea went nowhere, but Alison became increasingly aware that John had a deep-seated wish to do something to alleviate the difficulties of young people facing serious life challenges.

"What I believe," she says of John, "is that if you have had to struggle—starting with having to go to an East German orphanage during your youth, you want to share what you learned with others." She imagines John thinking, *Hey, I survived a difficult time. With the right attitude you can too.* "It makes sense to me," she says, "that this could lead him to help young people with addictions."

John would work in the garden, which she observed was therapy for him, and come back with ideas of what he should do. Maybe he should find out what's needed in Vancouver's infamous Downtown Eastside zone of poverty and addiction? Maybe he could provide free food? Maybe he should form a charitable organization? Maybe he should help fund others already there like the Salvation Army or the Union Gospel Mission. "I could tell he was spinning his wheels," says Alison looking back. "When we moved into the West Vancouver house, he started talking with foundations and boards, seeing what they were doing, taking baby-steps toward figuring out what he wanted to do. It didn't happen overnight. It was a learning process for him. It took years until he knew what he wanted to do."

As John flips through his photo albums that bracket the 2000 millennial year, his world of two decades ago returns. The photo shows John and Alison on a yacht off Deep Cove, BC, looking content in their matching nautical whites. There are photos of the kids hiking, skiing, and canoeing in British Columbia. And photos from a family trip to visit John's mother in Germany and later—after the Berlin Wall fell—to Arnstadt where John grew up. He stands with his children beneath the same Arnstadt window beneath which he and his two brothers posed fifty years before. In 2002: Uve, fourteen, is tall and lean; Talia, ten, has a short, bobbed haircut like her mother; and Lisanne, twelve, leans into her father affectionately. On another album page, John stands alone before a restored, half-timbered mansion in Eisenach, Germany, which had been his orphanage a half-century before.

John always wanted children—lots of children—and he loved them, doting on them as babies and admiring their independence and rebelliousness as they grew up. Uve is intelligent, spiritual and handsome and was always daring, ready to take risks. John recalls the time on a family trip to Germany when Uve challenged his father to give him fifty dollars if he were to jump into a castle's debris-filled moat. The moat was full of slime and rotting things.

"Uve, it could kill you."

"Come on, Dad. I'll do it for fifty dollars."

The jump never did happen, but Uve, now thirty-two years old, continues to be the daredevil—taking reckless chances and, on occasion, breaking bones. John recognized this impulsive behavior and suspected it might well be rooted in his own genes. "I was a risk-taker, too—it's what made me immigrate to Canada," he reflects. When drugs got the best of Uve, he paid for it with not one but two prison terms—lesson learned. He now catches up by being part of the team that builds the John Volken Academy Farm in Langley, BC. He is an example of a hard worker and is popular with all who know him. Uve is his dad's only son, and John loves him.

"It sounds so cliché to say that." Uve reflects, "my dad is my hero but I don't know how else to put it. I always felt loved and encouraged by him. His generosity, his love and respect towards people, his many successes and his ability to keep his ego in check; I've never seen it greater in any other human being. Now that I have a young son, I try to follow in my dad's footsteps; firm when it calls for it, and an unconditional love the rest of the time.

I know that one day if I end up a fraction of the man he is; I will die happy and content. Which is what I think we all want in the end."

Lisanne was his princess. She loves children. Her dad remembers when she excitedly pointed out at different places how cute the little ones were. One time, during a kindergarten parents' meeting, all the children were asked about what they wanted to be when growing up. All voiced their desired future profession except Lisanne; she answered with, "I want to be a mummy." John thought that was the best. Lisanne is now twenty-nine, married, and has three children . . . and there will be more . . . and she is still her dad's princess.

She admits that her father seldom talked about his German past. The children did, however, get glimpses of his youthful world during the family's European trips: the orphanage; the grandmother the children called "Oma"; and a reunion of old friends from the school that John had almost blown up. But they were kids then. The Eiffel Tower had a much greater appeal than tales of post-war East Germany. Lisanne admits, as well, that as a child she knew little about her father's United Furniture Warehouse business or his early efforts to build therapeutic communities. But by the time she was a teenager in the early 2000s, she was old enough to appreciate visiting Africa with her dad. He was setting up the Lift the Children charity, supporting ninety-two orphanages on that continent. Then there were the trips to rural Washington, where Lisanne and her siblings played in cold mountain streams; the summer trip to Alaska; and journeys to San Francisco, Spain, Portugal, and Las Vegas, where their father was baptized into the LDS church.

"As a young girl," Lisanne remembers, "my dad was everything I wanted him to be. He was a good provider, and was always there for me when I needed him. To the world, he was an accomplished businessman but to my brother, sister, and myself he was just our dad. When he was out of town, or worked late, he would always call to say goodnight. He was home every morning before school and Sundays. I have only fond memories of my dad, mostly from vacationing, him in the garden, or doing puzzles together. Now as an adult, I am proud of what my dad has accomplished and it's been admirable watching him continue to chase his dreams."

His younger daughter, Talia, had—and continues to have—the same maverick qualities, that both her dad and brother often displayed along with a little extra streak of stubbornness. John called her "Sunshine" as a child and remembers giving her a dancing mechanical doll that played the song he often sang to her: "You are my sunshine, my only sunshine . . . " Unlike her sister Lisanne, Talia was a tomboy and has become a much-travelled, free-spirited young woman. Her wanderlust, John suspects, may also be rooted in his genes. However, she is very reliable and is studying to be an accountant. Says John, "She is smart and will be a good one." John loves his children . . .

"As a teenager," Talia remembers "my dad was an easy-going parent that allowed me space to spend time with my friends and was always there for me when I needed him. He gave me the reins to develop my own choices and become my own person. He was always loving and caring.

He was, and still is, a hard-working individual, who has put a lot of time and passion into his work. He is an entrepreneur at heart, mind and soul, and will probably never stop working; even on his death bed. He's a smart, funny and stubborn man, who has a lot of love to give. He's accomplishing a lot in his lifetime; it's honestly hard to keep track of it all. I'm very proud to call him my dad. He's a good egg."

"John is very adventurous," says Alison of their marriage. "He's a 'Come on! Let's go! You can do it!' sort of guy. I remember in 1988, I was six-months pregnant with Uve, on an August trip to Europe. We rode a series of cable cars to the Zugspitze in the Alps, the 9,842-foot highest mountain in Germany. Everyone else was prepared and dressed in warm alpine clothes and boots. Not us. It was summer, and we were not prepared for the cold at the higher elevations. We were wearing summer clothes and sandals. There was crusted snow all the way to the summit. John led. I followed. I wasn't afraid. That's the way he is. 'Let's do it!' So, we did it."

And later, Alison recalls, her husband assumed the same energetic "Let's go!" enthusiasm on vacations with the kids. "We didn't just sit on the beach," she says. "Oh no. He's very hands-on. You rent a car and explore the area. You hop on the six o'clock tour bus. You go and see the orchid farm or whatever." But then, by late 2000, Alison disappears from the scene.

Amid his busy corporate life and at the beginning of his philanthropic activity, in 2001—despite efforts to reconcile—John found himself confronting divorce from his wife of thirteen years. Both John and Alison admit this was a wrenching time. The five horizontal meters of blue binders on the shelf adjacent to John's Surrey office testify to the divorce's legal entanglement—what exactly constituted Volken family assets, the financial claims against John's foundations, the years of court action, and $600-an-hour lawyers' fees. In the end, John sold United Furniture Warehouse (without the real estate assets) to The Brick furniture chain to resolve the seemingly endless legal case with Alison.

Says John of their divorce, "I suppose we just grew apart."

After the separation, the children continued to spend their weekends with their dad in his West Vancouver home. During school breaks they went on holiday trips. Those were exciting times—Alaska, France, Germany, Spain, Las Vegas, Grand Canyon, Knott's Berry Farm, the Splash Mountain roller coaster with John and his children screaming— the adventures are all captured in photos. But weekdays, the big house was no longer filled with the sounds of children. It was a challenging time for John. He decided to sell his house and move into a temporary place until his John Volken Academy complex in Surrey was ready. That is what happens too often to dreams.

Then entered Chawna into the picture, but that had to wait a few years.

CHAPTER 8

IT WAS A WHISPER, YET EVER SO CLEAR

...By Love Serve One Another[2]

By 1997, heroin addicts in Vancouver's Downtown Eastside were dying from drug overdoses at a rate of a hundred each year. Petty crime was rampant, HIV/AIDS was common from the sharing of needles, and the number of missing women had climbed toward thirty in the face of what seemed to be the actions of a serial killer of prostitutes. Thousands of residents lived in grim "single room occupancy" rooms and sought temporary escape through the drugs easily available in the neighborhood. The district's bleak, dumpster-filled back alleys were also lined with addicts, fixing heroin and smoking crack cocaine. Its street corners were equally full of young men who'd discreetly whisper to those passing by, "Up? Down?" as they peddled illicit drugs. It was the poorest neighborhood in Canada.

John witnessed the street people on the benches at Pigeon Park and lining up for food at the Union Gospel Mission and wondered how he could help those who needed help. "I had more money than I'd ever need," he says of that time. "For my family I'd built a $5.5 million home in West Vancouver. Being rich never was the objective. I like the challenge of 'making it.' My thoughts went back to East Germany. The lack

---

2   Galations 5:13

of freedom and the need for many of the things we take for granted in the USA and Canada allowed me to appreciate the amazing opportunities here and inspired me to share my good fortune and help feed the Downtown Eastside's needy." As a Christian, no passage in the Bible has inspired him more than *Matthew 25*. He quotes its words: "Inasmuch as ye have done it unto one of the least of these my brethren, ye have done it unto me." What a compelling call to action.

In 1997, John had hired a forty-six-year-old lawyer named Bilhar Koonar to be responsible for the leasing, buying, and constructing stores for United Furniture Warehouse. As it turned out, Bilhar was also a perfect fit for John's future endeavors. A second-generation Vancouverite of Punjabi ancestry, Bilhar had grown up on the periphery of the Downtown Eastside before it became a haven for drug addicts and the estranged. As a boy, he'd walked the streets going to movies there, unafraid. Over the years he had seen it all change. For three years he had been the president of the Boys and Girls Club of Greater Vancouver, so he had a heart for social issues. During the summer of 1998, Bilhar and John met with the people running the Salvation Army and Union Gospel to seek their advice on how best to help.

"I told them," John recalls, "I want to feed the poor." Their reply was not what I expected—they said, "There's lots of food around. What's needed is life skills and job skills to get them off the street.' They told me, 'We're detoxing people ten times or more by the time they're age thirty. The government won't give us long-term money. Short-term doesn't work. They go through detox and are told, 'Okay now you're clean. Get a life.' But they don't have the skills needed to do that. If you want to spend your money wisely—the kind of dollars you're talking about—if you can, set up a long-term, residential recovery program teaching life skills and job skills. That way you have a chance of stopping the rotation of people going in and out of detox.'"

Addiction treatment? Detox? Residential recovery? Life skills? John had little idea of what they were talking about.

To find out for himself what was going on, he ventured into the Downtown Eastside at night with a middle-aged woman named Mother Hastings. She wandered the streets, regularly handing out free sandwiches and potato salad—along with Christian blessings—to people on the side-walks and in the alleys. John gradually came to realize that the Salvation Army and Union Gospel people were correct. There was plenty of free food, but no opportunity for people to learn how to live healthy lives. Giving out food was not the answer. Arrests didn't work. Detox, in most cases, didn't work either. People would be back out on the street—and homeless—after a few weeks in prison or in detox and go immediately back to fixing again. Jail and detox just provided a revolving door for people caught in the vortex of their addictions. *To help—to really make a meaningful difference*, John thought, *there needs to be a program that teaches life skills and job skills to help them to become self-sustaining.*

In October 1998, John started planning a prospective facility to provide food, shelter, job, and life skills training for homeless people of the Downtown Vancouver Eastside. Back then, it was initially more of an idea, a wish, an amorphic concept, John acknowledges. There were a lot of things he would have to learn. But it was the beginning of the John Volken Academy and all that followed over the next twenty years.

During the years after John won the 1995 Entrepreneur of the Year Award, his main thoughts were redirected from building a moneymak-ing business to becoming a social entrepreneur. He talked with dozens of people involved in drug rehab and recovery programs. Most agreed that efforts at short-term drug detoxification programs simply do not work. Too many addicts return to their suppliers and bad habits shortly after their release, and many even relapse the same day. John had heard this on his walks with Vancouver's Mother Hastings while handing out sand-wiches at night. He'd heard it from social workers on the city's Downtown Eastside. He'd heard it from the young men in his small recovery house on Vancouver's Cambie Street in 2001. It all pointed in the direction that the long-term approach to recovery, including teaching a healthy lifestyle and an acceptable work ethic, is the most successful approach to lasting sobriety. John was determined to make this a reality.

He then set out on a lengthy series of journeys—to Los Angeles, New York, San Francisco, and Europe to gather pertinent information on how best to provide marginalized and addicted people with opportunities to escape their demons and turn their lives around.

He got his first glimpse of what a long-term, residential addiction rehabilitation and life skills facility, or a "therapeutic community" was all about. Until that time John had never even heard the name "therapeutic community," much less have any idea about what they did. But after learning about their methodology and success rate, he found it was the answer to what he wanted to do with his time and money.

Therapeutic Communities (TCs)

The term "therapeutic community" connotes a community that can remedy, restore, or cure. It is not a mental hospital or any other kind of hospital, but simply a place where struggling individuals overcome their demons and learn to become the best that they can be. The profound distinction between TCs and other treatment methods is that TCs go much further than simply helping individuals get sober—they teach a complete new lifestyle necessary to stay sober.

__TCs are group-based, highly structured, and powerful treatment approaches__ to addiction recovery. They provide a supportive environment where program participants change the destructive patterns they have developed that produced poor outcomes, and replace them with new attitudes, behaviors, and values that result in healthy living.

The TC motto __"Each one, Teach one"__ implies that individuals assume responsibility, not only for their own recovery, but also for the recovery of their peers. This, in turn, reinforces their own recovery. Personal growth and proper living are achieved by peers serving as role models, providing support through interaction, and confronting each other in group sessions.

__Program participants are expected to observe the behaviors and attitudes of their peers and take action to promote change__. The more senior participants teach by example and provide instruction and leadership. They act as big brothers and sisters to more junior members. They show them how to work, encourage them, reach out to them, "pull them in," monitor them, and correct their negative behaviors.

In a TC, program __participants are considered equals__ in their struggle to change their lives. While they have no formal authority over their peers, they have __considerable informal authority__ in their community management roles as they handle increasing amounts of responsibility. Junior members are primarily in roles where fewer demands are placed on them to lead. As they progress through the stages of the program, their attitudes and behaviors change, while their responsibility, accountability, and self-worth increase. This approach is so successful that there is no need for traditional psychiatrists or psychologists.

*Learning a totally new lifestyle cannot be achieved in a short-term program. To expect people with a history of addiction to turn their lives around and maintain sobriety after only a few months of treatment is simply unrealistic. This is why treatment at a TC lasts a minimum of two years—and often up to five years. This is another reason why therapeutic communities are the most effective way to achieve **lasting sobriety**.*

On that fact-finding mission through Europe, John stopped in to visit the city of the Umbrian region's most famous citizen, Saint Francis of Assisi. In the museum dedicated to Saint Francis, John explains, "I was overwhelmed by an unworldly, spiritual sensation I'd never quite experienced before. It confirmed my intent to help those who cannot help themselves."

John says of that experience, "Saint Francis came from wealth. When he had a spiritual awakening, he turned his back on money . . . and began a life of simplicity, abstinence, love, and the joys of nature." About missionary work he taught: 'Preach the gospel, at all times. When necessary, use words.' How inspiring!"

Back in Vancouver, equipped with a broader knowledge about therapeutic communities, John began putting shape to such a facility. He named it "Welcome Home." He spent $3.2 million purchasing a city block in Vancouver's industrial, low-income eastside. And—as newspaper accounts from that time testify—he hired an architectural firm to design an $18-million building for the site. He hoped to complete the facility by 2004. A newspaper headline at that time read, "Million-dollar man starts giving."

The seven-story, 130-bed complex was designed for young people— aged nineteen to twenty-four—struggling with addiction issues. John also vowed to create a substantial endowment fund to cover the facility's

$2-million annual operating cost. Living within the rigorous constraints and support of a therapeutic community, the students would stay there for a minimum of two years. They would be provided shelter, food, educational opportunities, job training, drug therapy, and instruction in nutritional and social skills. All this on condition that the residents abide by the Welcome Home rules: no drugs, no alcohol, no threats or swearing, no violence.

There were doubters and critics. While most admitted the urgent need for a place to provide BC youth with shelter and drug therapy, there were those in the Downtown Eastside who questioned John's lack of experience in dealing with addiction. Good intentions, they said, do not necessarily translate into workable deeds. There were others who suspected that the massive scale of the project would ultimately dwarf other smaller facilities in the area, cutting into their financial support by leaving them smaller pieces of the seldom-generous social services' pie. Vancouver's Planning Department argued that because of noise, heavy traffic, and surrounding factories, the proposed location for the Welcome Home facility did not suit the city's industrial land-use plans.

The City of Vancouver made him spend over $50,000 to cover the cost of a delegation to visit similar facilities in San Francisco, Los Angeles, and New York. The report came back positive, but Vancouver city planners declined John's proposal anyway. In fact one bureaucrat said, "Take your big bucks and go somewhere else."

Said John of the opposition, "Imagine! Why did they make me spend $50,000 and then disregard the positive report and decline the proposal? After all the research we'd done, after all the money we'd already spent and our readiness to invest in a much-needed cause, how could anyone with a sincere desire to change those broken lives fight such a paid-for solution?"

John was beginning to learn that trying to establish a facility for the treatment of drug addicts anywhere produces an almost inevitable NIMBY (Not In My Back Yard) effect. This negative reaction is experienced by almost all who want to build similar establishments. He would encounter this again before Welcome Home established itself in Surrey, BC.

He sold the $3.2 million city block and bought a duplex on Cambie Street in Vancouver. Within a few weeks he was housing about twenty street people. Again there was a NIMBY effect. An elderly lady next door frantically complained to the mayor and tried everything to stop the project. However, within a short time, when she got to know the young men, she baked cookies for them. But the place was small, just a duplex. Surrey was a different story. There were signs and protest, but the city council approved the zoning change with a plea: "We voted for you, but please don't disappoint us."

They weren't disappointed.

In Phoenix AZ, John's foundation bought a large house in an established neighborhood. When the people held a hearing in a neighborhood park, it was more like a hostile riot with municipal leaders present. John's plan was shouted down—literally. At the end, it was a blessing in disguise. He sold the house and bought a forty-acre ranch in nearby Gilbert—which served its purpose much better.

But regardless of those many disappointing efforts, there were equally as many mayors, councillors, and members of the general public who were supportive—even enthusiastic—in their support for John's causes. But in general, reflecting on those early challenges, John says of his initial efforts to establish Welcome Home, "Hypocrisy comes to mind. People profess to care, but when it comes time to act they would rather play it safe and stick to the status quo. To say: 'Take your big bucks and go someplace else' while thousands of young men and women overdose every day. They lacked the political fortitude to step out of the box, even though what they were saying and half-heartedly doing wasn't working."

With an edge of annoyance in his voice, John adds, "No question about it, it seems to be more of a challenge to give money away and make a positive impact than it is to make money." But he counts himself blessed that roadblocks only give you experience. "The results make it all worth it."

God does not expect us to succeed.
He expects us to do the best that we can do.
Mother Theresa

A satellite view of Surrey, BC on Google Maps shows the province's second-largest city as mostly grey and residential in its northern half and green with farms and forests where it borders the USA. Located southeast of Vancouver, Surrey is a classic example of late-twentieth-century urban sprawl—with its attendant numbered streets and avenues of middle-class homes yielding to cultivated agricultural land and hobby ranches at its extremities. In fact, Surrey's population has tripled to 520,000 since 1988. Cutting from north to south through Surrey is the 9.5-mile-long King George Boulevard, a four-lane highway lined with strip malls, big-box stores, fast-food chains, and street-side parking lots. Zoom the aerial view farther down onto the intersection of 68th Avenue and King George Boulevard and there—in the southernmost block of the highway's solid retail development—is a district called Newton. This is where an empty ex-United Furniture store stood, which John used for his first addiction recovery facility.

It is not a simple thing to spend $64 million. But that's what it has cost the John Volken Foundation to acquire the land adjacent to that first facility, along with the construction of the complete complex that now occupies the 8.5-acre site. The money came from the sale of several ex-United Furniture stores held by the John Volken Foundation. Fourteen houses were bought and demolished, and this land, together with bare land next to it, became the future home of the John Volken Academy.

As the land assembly and architectural renderings were happening, John's plan to establish a long-term facility for people going through drug addiction rehabilitation became a political football in Surrey. There were neighborhood protests and petitions circulated that culminated in a public hearing at Surrey's City Council between John and his allies, and angry NIMBY opponents to the JVA proposal. Views were heard and councillors were threatened with election defeat. But in the end, with much of Mayor Dianne Watts's coaching, the plan was overwhelmingly approved—with only one dissenting vote.

The Academy includes a 100-plus unit dormitory for program par-ticipants and an attached, multi-purpose, classroom-gym-workshops-administrative building. This is where JVA students eat, attend classes, go through group therapy, exercise, and socialize. Between these two build-ings sits an extravagant flower and tree-filled garden. And next to that is the PricePro supermarket/furniture store, where the JVA students learn to work as a team and develop new skillsets, crafting them into valuable employees. To the immediate west of the site, a row of eight residential homes were bought for almost $1 million each to provide housing for female students and to serve as transition homes for JVA graduates.

But it didn't take John and his JVA associates long to discover a couple of challenges in trying to establish a therapeutic community in Vancouver. In the well-established facilities in Europe and North America he'd visited, many types of job skills training were available. What activities would be available at the soon-to-be built JVA site in Surrey?

The decision was made to build a big-box supermarket that would be located next door to the JVA buildings and contain upstairs classrooms, administrative offices, and John's apartment. A full-service supermarket, including a furniture and mattress department, meant that students could learn meat-cutting, baking, warehouse management, accounting, marketing, graphic design, salesmanship, and most importantly, gain an acceptable work ethic all under one roof. These departments would be managed by paid, professional butchers, bakers, and accountants, hired with the knowledge that they'd be working with students from the John Volken Academy.

In September 2009, the John Volken Academy's 60,000-square-foot big-box PricePro supermarket opened, staffed by twenty JVA students enrolled at that time, its purpose being to provide hands-on work experience and training for students enrolled in the academy. Most departments are run by trained staff whose dual jobs are to run the store and to teach the JVA student-apprentices skills that might qualify them for jobs once they have graduated. A few departments are run by former students, who after graduation have assumed paid management positions. In this way, the store is, in fact, a school. The sign out front on busy King George Boulevard suggests what the place is all about. It reads:

PRICEPRO
Save Money/Change Lives

The signs inside PricePro, hanging from the ceiling and echoed on the walls reiterate the uniqueness of the supermarket/school:

Canada's only not-for-profit supermarket

> Feel great. All proceeds go to charity.
> Thank you for helping change lives.
> Enjoy Saving Money.

Gabrielle Steed, aged forty, has volunteered with the John Volken Academy for two years. She held a teaching position in a Burnaby, BC secondary school, and as a member of the JVA Advisory Committee, made her mark by getting things done. She was a doer. When a decision was reached to develop an idea, or gather information, or whatever it was, she was the one who did it. Promptly too. It impressed John and he cornered her one day with: "Did you ever think about doing this full time?" She was frustrated with the school system and impressed with the JVA program. However, the starting remuneration of what John offered did not quite match the salary, health, and pension plan of the school board. That is why the answer, "Let me think about it," almost surprised John more than when a few days later she accepted the offer. That was in 2009 and until her departure in 2018, she was JVA's Vice-President of Education (and unofficial doer-of-everything-that-must-get-done in an operation involving three JVA facilities and their advisory committees).

Gabrielle explains the role PricePro plays in the running of the Academy. "Most of the PricePro departments are staffed by licensed professionals. The PricePro bakery has a professional baker. The students working there are not just learning how to be bakers, they're actually logging hours for the food industry's training authority. They're getting their bakery certification. PricePro is the school in British Columbia, the JVA Ranch is the school in Arizona, and PriceCo is the school in Washington. Somebody might say, 'Oh, that is where they make addicts work, and they don't pay them.' Well, no. It costs well over $150,000 every month, plus the cost of the facilities, for the students to be there. They're getting their education, their housing, their food, their therapy—for a minimum of two years—in a safe community environment of peers. And when they graduate, they've got marketable skills."

In practical terms, the overall management of the PricePro store falls to sixty-one-year-old Mark Pitcher, whose job description includes supervising the current sixty JVA students and their responsibilities. The students circulate through different departments—working the cash registers, driving warehouse forklifts, practicing the techniques of butchering, or designing advertising, learning the art of baking, dealing with wholesalers—until they settle into a job that might provide them with future employment. Pitcher is a professional baker whose career began in Victoria, BC, where he learned his culinary skills and applied them, decades ago, at the Salvation Army's Addiction Recovery Center.

"I really loved what I was doing at the Salvation Army, but I had a problem with the way their short-term program was almost like a revolving door. I wanted them to succeed. But it wasn't working, and it was taking a toll on me."

With the desire to do something meaningful with his culinary skills, he took the job of running the PricePro bakery in 2017 and was soon running the entire supermarket. Pitcher is also responsible for running the Academy's in-house kitchen, where a half-dozen JVA students plan nutritionally balanced meals, prepare ingredients, cook, and serve three meals a day to their co-students. Pitcher also supervises PricePro's catering service and snack bar where other students acquire food-service skills.

"We're all about training," says Pitcher as he surveys the vast supermarket and its staff of busy, clean-cut, JVA-logo-wearing students. Only the signs on the walls and hanging overhead would give any indication that the store is unique, and that the young men and women there are actively working to escape a past life of drugs, depression, crime, thoughts of suicide, and hopelessness.

Working in PricePro with young men and women who have survived years of serious addiction, Pitcher testifies, requires a high level of compassion and patience. "As John keeps repeating," says Pitcher of his boss, "'Don't like the behavior, but love the individual.' That will go a long way. John expects his staff to be role models and examples for the students. He expects us to be able to not only teach them new skills to live by but to show them what they can aspire to become: to have a family, a career, a home, and to become valuable citizens, and yes, be a taxpayer. Instead of being 'takers' they become 'givers' and 'contributors.'"

It had been a twenty-year journey for John since he'd first considered selling United Furniture Warehouse after receiving the Entrepreneur of the Year Award in 1995, and he asked himself, *Well, what do I do now?*

On April 24, 2015, the famous philosopher and writer, Deepak Chopra, took the stage at the grand opening of the new, $64-million John Volken Academy in Surrey and spoke on addiction and how it works. "Everyone has a predisposition to some form of addiction," he said. "It's not just substances. Addiction's a memory so strong—usually a memory of pleasure—that a person has an inability to escape it." The goal of getting free of one's addictions, Chopra explained, is to stop creating divisions between what's in the mind and in the body and in the person's spirit. "Whatever happens in the mind is recorded in the body. And whatever happens in the body is recorded in the mind." The addiction gets embedded there—in the person's mind and body and spirit. The goal of treatment is to reach a deeper level of consciousness—a "slow peeling off of the addictive tendencies."

Chopra's philosophic perspective on addiction echoes the guiding principles of the long-term approach to the treatment of addiction within the John Volken Academy. The "slow peeling off" can occur only over a substantial amount of time—as JVA students deal with the mental, physical, emotional, social, spiritual, financial, and vocational aspects of living well, free of former drug and alcohol abuse.

After Chopra's speech, John talked about the fundamental purpose of his academy " . . . to save and change lives . . . everybody has a song to sing and they cannot sing it as addicts . . . the focus and mission of this academy is to help every student to become the very best that he or she can be . . . "

The two men then walked to the JVA's foyer armed with two pairs of scissors—and with John's wife, Chawna, smiling behind them—cut the ribbon, officially opening the 215,000-square-foot John Volken Academy.

CHAPTER 9

A NEW BEGINNING
Love Finds Its Way Again

In the years before and after 2000, John was adding up to twenty stores a year to his business. By 2003, there were 152 United Furniture stores in North America, about 101 in Canada and fifty-one in the USA. At that time, UFW produced over $200 million in annual sales and $10 million in annual profits.

Moving in tandem with this growth strategy was John's initiative in 1997 to fund his foundations in the USA and Canada. The real-estate holdings in the USA were transferred into the USA John Volken Foundation, and the Canadian stores were transferred into the John Volken Foundation Canada. With the real estate owned by the foundations, the monthly rents paid by tenants provided the foundations with the needed cash flow to support John's philanthropic endeavors.

In 1990, Chawna Naito, her husband Shu, and their two children (with one on the way) arrived in Vancouver from Hawaii. Shu was being transferred as an executive for Coast hotels. Chawna had been born Chawna Brown in Scottsdale, Arizona—into a large Church of Jesus Christ of Latter Day Saints family. Chawna and Shu had met and married while attending Brigham Young University in Provo, Utah. Soon after arriving in Canada, the Naitos bought a home in North Vancouver and began attending the local LDS congregation, which the Volkens also attended. Life was busy with young children and hectic careers, and the two families didn't interact much except to say hello in passing in the hallways.

Fast forward ten years. Now with five children, the Naito family moved to Coquitlam, a part of the greater Vancouver area, and lost contact with the Volkens. One day, though, Chawna and Shu appeared in Coquitlam's United Furniture Warehouse store. John recalls:

> It was the company's head office and main store, and I was, coincidentally, on the sales floor that day. I knew that there had been some marital difficulties between Chawna and her husband, but their appearance together, shopping for furniture, suggested that it had been resolved. We talked kindly, and I was happy to see them together. I knew firsthand how difficult divorce could be, with my divorce being filed the previous year. I didn't know that Chawna and Shu were, in fact, separated and trying to have an amicable relationship for the sake of their children.
>
> A few years later, on a winter Saturday afternoon, after a tubing sleigh ride party, a youth group came to my house for hot chocolate. My house was large, and I enjoyed the company. I had run into the Naito family the week prior and invited them to join the party too. While on the drive over from Coquitlam, Chawna and Shu had a disagreement that resulted in Shu leaving the party early. Chawna and her twins were left stranded at the party. During the course of the evening, I'd had the opportunity to speak with Chawna about life and its ups and downs, which eventually led to the topic of divorce. I told her how I didn't believe in divorce, and with all the conviction I could muster I tried to talk her out of it. Little did I know, that conversation motivated her to give her marriage another chance, something she is still grateful for. Even though her marriage ended in divorce a few years later, that extra time proved very healing for

her and her family. Chawna went on to get her real-estate license and forged a new path in her life.

On the very first day that forty-four-year-old Chawna received her real-estate license in December 2004, her Keller Williams Realty boss advised her to start calling people she knew to let them know about her new career. From an earlier conversation at church, she understood that John had recently sold his elegant Farmleigh Road home and was looking for a temporary place to rent until his apartment above the John Volken Academy in Surrey was completed. She also knew, from casual conversation at church, that he'd been delaying for quite a while in making a decision about where to go or what to do house-wise. Now the timeline was to be a few weeks. In the meantime, he needed a temporary place for himself, his son, and his two daughters, plus storage for the furniture from his 14,000-square-foot home.

When John realized the urgency of signing a lease for a temporary abode, he talked to a friend about it: "I have to move out of my 'palace' within a month, and still have to find a place to move to."

He thought it was funny when his friend quipped, "John, you are the richest homeless person I know." Humor yes, but John's friend was partly right. John had to act quickly.

That's when Chawna saved the day. "I knew he had to sign a rental contract almost immediately because his "house on the hill" was sold, and he had to move within thirty days. I thought if I could quickly find a vacant home that someone wanted to sell fast, maybe he would buy it. I plugged all the criteria into my computer—like 'vacant possession'—and got a number of local listings. I then ran the printer and left the file— with some purchase possibilities—on John's West Vancouver doorstep. That night, when he got home, he found the file folder."

John remembers: "When I got home and first saw the file, I thought it was a waste of time for Chawna. Until the construction of the new John Volken Complex with my apartment was completed, I wanted to rent, not buy. But when I started looking through the file, I saw a home that looked interesting. I called her and she set up an appointment to see it the next evening."

"The next evening, we went to view the house on North Vancouver's Capilano Road," Chawna recalls, picking up the story's thread. "We looked around . . . and he bought the house on the spot. Just like that. It was actually dark. We couldn't even see what the backyard looked like or anything. It was the only house we looked at. It was a crazy deal for me. I had gotten my license the day before. My first showing. No subjects. All cash. Done! I didn't even know what I was doing."

John recalls, "A few days later, it turned out the buyer of 'my house on the hill' didn't have the funds to close the deal. Now I had two houses and the 'would-be buyer' lost his $500,000 deposit. I resold the house several months later and had plenty of time to move into my new, temporary house. It worked out perfectly. Furthermore, the apartment in Surrey, instead of only taking a few months, wasn't ready for another three years. I would never have survived in any of those apartments I had looked at. The furniture alone wouldn't have fit . . ."

During that time Chawna, as a friendly colleague, was also introduced to the academy's students. She says of that time: "In my mind, drug addicts were people to avoid and stay away from. Because of having no experience of being around people who were drug addicts or from prison, I was scared to death of them. So I thought, *It's great he has the heart to help them. It's really awesome of John.* I'd sit in on those meetings and just listen to him, and I began to realize how passionate he was for the students to change. Little by little, I just kind of really warmed up to the fact that drug addicts needed more love and understanding than most people."

Chawna continues, "John is all about overcoming obstacles, handling challenges, and extending forgiveness and love. I knew he missed having a wife and loved the time he had with his children. I thought, *He deserves a really good woman. I'm going to find him the perfect wife.* So, as a caring friend, I was always trying to find dates for him, trying to be a match-maker. 'Let's sign you up on eHarmony,' I'd tell him. I remember one day my mother called. I told her I was trying to fix John up and asked, 'Mom, do you know of any really amazing women that are available?'

"She said, 'Oh yeah, there are a lot of single women down here in Arizona.' And then she warned, 'Well, Chawna, you do realize when he does find this woman, the new wife will probably not want you to be a part of his life?'

"That was probably the first time it hit me," Chawna recalls. "I remember it hurt me to think that somebody could try to ruin the friendship I had with John. I thought: *There's no way that could happen!*"

The thought lingered:

> I really admired what John was doing. He was choosing to help people who couldn't help themselves, and he was not asking anything from them except to follow a program for better mental health and, in time, heal. I loved that. And I began to see, in time, that I couldn't really separate the work from the man, as his heart was all in.
>
> John's pretty forward and determined. When he wants something, he goes after it. But he never gave me any vibe, never made any type of advances, and I was fine with that. I felt really, really safe . . . like he was a protective brother. I had no foresight, no idea—that our relationship would turn romantic.
>
> One day we were just talking on the phone. Somehow the conversation got into our hopes and our dreams, and he asked me what I wanted in life. I said, you know, the normal things: I want to be happy. I want my children to be happy. And so, of course, then I asked him the same question: What are you wanting in life? And his answer was, "I want you."
>
> I didn't have a response. I was too surprised. I knew that I felt very safe with John, and I definitely knew that I didn't want another woman severing our relationship down the road. I knew I wanted him in my life. But it was such a big jump from him being one of my best friends to marriage. So I just said, "Ummm, can I think about it?" because I needed to think about it.
>
> Here's the cool thing about John: Most men would be impatient with that kind of an answer. They would

question why the feelings weren't immediately recip-
rocated and might lose motivation. But John was like,
"Sure, take all the time you need." He knew this was a big
leap for both of us.
We'd never even held hands. Nothing! Zero! And I'm
asking myself, how do we go from being best friends to
suddenly considering a life together?
I realized then that I had developed a love for him without
knowing it. So my answer was, "Yes, I love you. I want to
be with you, too."

John and Chawna were married on September 8, 2006. The date was
agreed on while he was with his three children in Germany. The location
was in a beautiful West Vancouver home owned by long-time friends of
John—the Cunninghams. John had a tulip on his lapel. Chawna wore a
white headband that matched John's white hair. And the next day they
moved into the North Vancouver house she'd sold her husband-to-be two
years earlier.

Their honeymoon was a cruise to Mexico. Four days into the trip,
Chawna excitedly announced she had found a Japanese sushi station,
something John had never eaten. From the buffet, Chawna piled servings
of exquisite sushi rolls and sashimi onto her plate, and John followed,
loading up his plate with unfamiliar selections. Moments after they sat
down in the ship's crowded restaurant, John's face—from Chawna's perspective—assumed a look of terror. He jumped out of his chair, grabbed
his head on both sides, and started bobbing up and down. His eyes looked
like they were popping out. For a moment, Chawna was certain he was
having a brain aneurism and that these could be her final moments with
him. But as quickly as he had jumped up, he sat down, shook his head and
simply said, "What was that?" He pointed toward a mound of green on
his plate, indicating he'd just eaten a whole spoonful. Being on a Mexican
cruise, unfamiliar with Japanese cuisine, he'd mistaken the buffet's fiery
wasabi mustard for guacamole. To this day, John and Chawna still laugh
at the story.

John's temporary new house in North Vancouver was a happy home. Every second Friday through Sunday, his three children—Talia then twelve years old; Lisanne, fourteen; and Uve, sixteen—made it their home. Each child had their own room. The rest of the time they lived with their mother in White Rock, about thirty miles away. John's house became a popular gathering place for their friends. He learned to cook awesome spaghetti and sundried tomatoes sour chicken. Everyone loved it.

The home became an even happier place when his new wife Chawna joined him there in 2006. Now it was a family home. John says, "Although we each have our own children, it's been a joy for me to have Chawna's five children in addition to my own. Each of her children have worked for me over the years, and I hope I've taught them something as well—they are all hardworking, productive citizens. I'm proud of them. Now I'm a grandfather too, so that's also fun!"

About four years later, in 2009, the new John Volken Academy complex in Surrey was completed. John and Chawna sold the house and moved to Surrey into an apartment at the John Volken Academy, right where his work was. A few years later they bought an apartment in North Vancouver as their official residence.

When asked, "Why Chawna?" John smiles and recounts: I knew her for years. We both were married and had a family. We attended the same church, and I always noticed her as a very beautiful lady, but that was all. When I went through my divorce, Chawna was still married, so she was not part of the dating scene. Once she was divorced, we spent time together and became friends.

I noticed things about her I never observed when she was married. She is intelligent and charming, sociable and beautiful, humble and loyal, sometimes a little naïve. I like that too; perhaps it makes me feel more needed. Best of all, she cares for and loves me. In February 2019, I could see it in her face when I fell off a rock formation and broke my femur and wrist. I couldn't move, and it was somewhat reassuring and very comforting to observe her terrified expression and tears. Ever since then, she doesn't want me to go anywhere by myself in case something happens to me.

She cares, not just about me, but about anything and anybody that needs caring for. She attends most of my meetings, accompanies me on many of my trips to Africa, and supports my efforts there. She knows every JVA student by name and their history. She often talks about her father whenever something reminds her of him. He died a few years ago of leukemia—but he was and still is one of her idols. It has been said that the way a woman treats her father is the way she will treat her husband . . . She is sixty and I am eighty, so whenever we talk about the long-term future, she gets visibly sad. I could go on, but it is enough. In short: I am a lucky man."

Chawna quickly adds, "I really never think about our age difference because John is so high-energy and driven. I love his passion to help change lives, as well as his commitment to help those who can't help themselves."

1951 With our mother.
From left: Roger, Bernd & John.

1952: Christmas with my favourite
cousin Juergen.

1953: The three of us from left: Bernd (13yrs), John (11yrs) and Roger (10yrs).

1953
Countries, continent and ocean apart. True friendship knows no border or time.
From left: Hartmut, Peter & John.   From left: Peter, Klaus & John.

2010

Sept. 2, 1960
The day before leaving for Canada.
From left, My older brother Bernd,
I am next in my treasured leather pants,
my younger brother Roger and my
mother.

Sept. 3, 1960
At 18 I am off to Canada!
I just said goodbye to friends and family,
who took me to Bremerhaven and waved
as the ship started towards Halifax,
Nova Scotia. No tears, but lots of
enthusiasm (and hair!).

1964: My first return visit to Germany.
My friend James.   With my brothers from left: Bernd, Roger, John.

Squandering time in Las Vegas 1966-1968

The classic Sands Hotel, with 715 rooms, was one of my favorite Las Vegas landmarks. Frank Sinatra and the Rat Pack were headliners. Sheldon Adelson, one of the richest men in America, bought the famed hotel in 1989, demolished it in 1996 to make way for the Venetian Resort Hotel with 4049 rooms.

For two years in Vegas, I stayed in the Towne & Country Motel on Fremont Street for $60 per month. It had a pool, the management was friendly and the rooms were clean.

In 2021 this Motel still looks the same. Many (many) times I took the 25 min walk at night to gamble in downtown and did not get home until morning.

During my stay in Las Vegas and beyond, my Volkswagen Bug served me faithfully. Those were exciting times...I thought then. How one's thinking can change!

For 20 years the freezer food business was an 'on again, off again' enterprise that always produced a good profit. Starting in 1964 as a salesman for Domestic Foods in North Bay, Ontario, next was Burmount Foods during the early 1970's and Westland Foods during the late 70's.

In between the freezer food business there were other ventures like the clothing stores Threadsetters (1973), the book mail order business (1976) and about half a dozen others, all providing a satisfying financial return. But none could hold my interest for long until I conceived the idea of a buying and selling service that could expand worldwide. Now that was exciting. It started in 1981 as United Buy and Sell Service...

97

1961. Top left clockwise:
      I got my feet wet in business;
      "Jahn's Flower Shop". A great,
      early learning experience!

1981. The humble beginning of United
      Furniture Warehouse.

1991. With general manager David
      Gerstner in front of United
      Furniture Warehouse's head office
      and store.

1995. My acceptance speech at the
      Entrepreneur Of The Year
      Award celebration.

1995
The West Vancouver home under construction with my children helping.
From left, Uve (7yrs), Talia (3yrs), Lisanne (5yrs).

1998
It took 5 years to build the home that was supposed to last forever. The finished product was beautiful.

Happy days with Alison...

The five of us in front of the new home with our children. From left: Talia, Lisanne & Uve.

2001

...and then there were only four of us.

In the wild....

...on vacation, in Europe...

...or during special events.

There was always lots of happiness and love

2006
...and then there were 10 of us. In front of our North Vancouver home. From left: Uve, Brandt, Bryce, Stephen. Back row from left: Brooke, Talia, Chawna, John, Lisanne, Stephanie.

September 8, 2006
I am signing my life
away....happily.
It's Chawna forever!
My friend, dentist
and bishop, Dr. Thomas
Walker performed the
wedding and is watching
as we are signing...

On that special day with my
long-time friends, Ross and
Helen Cunningham in their
home in West Vancouver.
For many years Ross was
president of A&W
restaurants - he did well.
She is a quintessential host
and an incredible cook.

...and off we go!

CHAPTER 10

IF IT'S GOOD, LET IT GROW
A Life of Philanthropy

As John established his therapeutic facility in Surrey, BC, in the early 2000s, the next step was to expand into the USA.

In 2003, John bought a beautiful older home in Seattle, Washington, to serve as the first dorm in the USA. A vacant ex-United Furniture Warehouse store became the training center. Every morning and evening, students were bussed to and from the center. Two years later, the first USA students graduated. It was a humble beginning—but it didn't take long for the program to grow.

In 2010, he bought a large, out-of-business furniture store in Kent, Washington. He remodeled it to serve as a furniture and mattress store in which future students would learn warehousing, administration, and other job skills. He named it PriceCo. On the same property, a three-story dorm was built to be the home for up to seventy students.

The John Volken Academy complex on Kent's busy North Central Avenue sits amid a lengthy stretch of car lots, apartment buildings, strip malls, and warehouses in a suburban community halfway between Seattle and Tacoma. By 2018, it had become home to about fifty JVA students, all young men, whose work-related training encompasses the furniture store, a moving company (Academy Movers), a lawn service (Academy Lawn Services), and a woodworking shop.

Terri Conger, chairwoman of the Kent Advisory Committee, says of the JVA students, "The students come here in pain. Some come from disintegrating families. Some come from wealthy families and have grown up with easy consumerism. Here, they find themselves in a safe, structured environment. The core program is disciplined and regimented. They're held accountable for their behavior. It's not easy. But it's done with love and respect. It's joyful to watch the students change. They are among the most tenacious and committed young men I've ever met."

In 2012, John acquired a 39.5-acre ranch in Gilbert, Arizona, located at the southernmost edge of Phoenix's suburban perimeter. He paid $1.9 million for the ranch, an awesome price, even during the real estate lull (the property without any improvements is worth $12 million after ten years) and, with $8 million more, the property was upgraded to be the Arizona home of the John Volken Academy. The ranch lies adjacent to the Sun Groves housing development on one side, the Gila River Indian Community on another, and the Sonoran Desert, which stretches south to the distant San Tan Mountains. Enclosed within the property are a covered riding arena, a riding school, a horse pool, stables, sheds for farm equipment, chicken coops and pig pens, and of course residences and classrooms for the students working on overcoming their addictions and learning job and life skills. Unlike the sites in Kent and Surrey, which are both focused on retail stores and services training, the Gilbert site maintains a ranching and agricultural environment. The chickens produce eggs, the pigs and cattle give meat, and the greenhouse and garden generate vegetables. The main income for the ranch, however, comes from boarding and taking care of about 150 horses. The ranch is also the home of the Gilbert Rodeo, a yearly, three-day event with competitions and spectators attending from all over Arizona and beyond. It is the largest rodeo in the Phoenix area.

Carson Brown, aged forty, chairman of the JVA's Arizona Advisory Committee, had seen a wealthy Phoenix neighborhood rise up in protest at John's first, failed effort to establish the academy in Arizona. The misguided NIMBY sentiment predates all or most rehabilitation establishments, no matter how well they are run or how they may even enhance the neighborhoods. John was relieved that the Gilbert location received the green light with less acrimonious acceptance in 2012—although only after many, many re-zoning hearings, special-use applications, and public meetings.

Carson got involved with the JVA through John marrying his sister, Chawna. He remembers visiting the academy in Canada with his wife Jennifer and staying in Volken's apartment at the John Volken Academy. After their first day there, his wife asked, "When am I going to meet some of the drug addicts?"

To which John responded, "You've been meeting them all day."

She hadn't realized the polite, smiling, well-dressed clerks and cashiers in the PricePro store were, in fact, the formerly grim "drug addicts" of her imagination. Says Carson, "It hit me then. This place is really different," and with this, he started to work with his brother-in-law to open a therapeutic community in Arizona. Carson and John's persuasive wife Chawna convinced John to buy the ranch in Gilbert, and they all helped it to get established.

From Carson's subsequent conversations with the Gilbert JVA students, he has come to understand that, by his estimate, a large percentage of the young men there have been drawn into their addictions through prescription drugs. "They often start with painkillers and move on to heroin," he says. "When the students first enter the program they are often broken. They're put to work outdoors—with animals, with nature, with the earth. They get dirty, sweaty, take a shower, and can say, 'Hey, I accomplished something today.' Working outdoors with the horses, it's really therapeutic."

Carson knows the students well. He has introduced more struggling young men and women to the JVA than any other person. He visits the ranch often and helps the students in their struggles to adopt a new life.

Carson works for Conley Wolfswinkel, a successful Arizona land developer. Wolfswinkel, together with his staff, is very supportive of the JVA. Carson and Seth Keeler, his co-worker, have volunteered many hours bolstering the cause of the JVA. "Seth is one of the most Christ-like and effective people I know," says John.

For John to administer the three JVA facilities—one in the Vancouver area, one 120 miles south of Vancouver in Kent, WA, and one 1,200 miles south of Vancouver in Gilbert, AZ—requires the energy that few have, especially a man of his age. Those around him report that his ability to juggle a dozen different tasks simultaneously is simply unbounded. The word "workaholic" is discreetly mentioned, but never in his presence. He takes stairs two-at-a-time. He runs meetings, deals with invoices and checks, teaches JVA classes, and oversees the two stores, the ranch in Gilbert, and the new, expanding farm in Langley, BC. In a daily rush of activity, he hires new staff; chats up employees, local politicians, and parents of potential students; conducts interviews and gives speeches; and straightens wall-mounted pictures that have become slightly unaligned. Curiously, he finds himself feeling guilty. "I should be doing something productive!" he often tells himself at the prospect of watching a lazy hour of TV with his loving wife to unwind before going to bed, mostly at 2:00 a.m. or later.

Here, according to his assistant, Gabrielle Steed, is what a man of seventy-eight does when he's slowing down: "When he goes to Kent: he works in his Surrey complex till about noon, leaves Vancouver at 2:00 p.m., drives three hours or so south, checks in with the PriceCo manager, drops off checks, collects invoices, and enjoys a meal with the students, followed by an advisory committee meeting. The next morning, he has breakfast with the students at 7:15 a.m., then a Student Council/Training Meeting where the Kent staff and senior students discuss JVA policies, operational procedures, and student advancements. Then it's supper, followed by a two-hour interaction with the students during the 'Message for Life' session. The next day, the facility is inspected, which involves training meetings and appointments. At 7:00 p.m., it's 'My Challenge Night,' where he gets students with particularly challenging issues to talk about themselves. Answers are found and challenges issued. He leaves around 10:00 p.m. and drives back to Vancouver, two and a half hours north."

"It's a whirlwind," says Steed, who sometimes has accompanied him on these jaunts. "Forty-eight hours, almost non-stop. He does the same thing each month with Arizona. Only he flies and is gone for five or six days. On the ranch, the day starts with breakfast at 5:15 a.m. Then the same thing: checks, invoices, council meeting, advisory committee meeting, group therapy sessions, training sessions, interviews, and mentoring the students during the John Volken Night. He presents a subject like honesty, courage, self-acceptance, adversity, forgiveness, service . . . whatever. It is always interactive, and students are encouraged to participate. These evenings are very enjoyable for both John and the students. The next night, he facilitates 'My Challenge Night', where he focuses on students with special challenges.

In 2018, Steed left to become a full-time mother. She is missed but has been replaced by a very qualified woman named Jane Terepocki. She says, "Unlike most philanthropists, whose generosity is primarily shown through giving money, John is a hands-on philanthropist. Living within the Surrey facility, he interacts on a daily basis with the students and staff in the Surrey JVA: teaching classes; hiring and training staff; discussing managerial issues; planning events; running council meetings, manager meetings, and advisory committee meetings; chatting with potential incoming students and encouraging students who are struggling on their path of changing their lives; designing landscaping; helping with the gardening; or deciding on the flagpole location. This same hands-on involvement is repeated in his monthly or bi-monthly visits to the facilities in Washington and Arizona, where he maintains regular contact and instructional roles with the students and staff."

John has to prepare the agendas for all those meetings, and everyone expects the topics and meetings to be meaningful. Plus, with 150 students in three places, John says, "The students expect me to know their names and their history. I always had challenges in remembering names. My wife tells me many times: 'Don't call anyone by name.' She has a point—it is embarrassing when I don't get it right. But being so involved may keep me from getting Alzheimer's," he says with a smile. "I am just grateful to be healthy and to be able to do the work."

In 2014, at a special occasion in Vancouver, BC, John received from His Holiness the Dalai Lama, the Humanitarian Award for his philanthropic efforts with North American drug addicts. The Dalai Lama Centre's testimonial cited his dedication to providing life-changing opportunities for addicts who might otherwise never glimpse the possibilities of good health and success.

The final paragraph of the testimonial reads: "John is a role model for all of society, exemplified in part by his modest lifestyle. He leads a life completely devoid of opulence and extravagance. He is a constant reminder to us, his students, and those he cares for, of the importance of simplicity, moderation, and giving."

CHAPTER 11

A MEMORABLE EVENING
The Cufflinks

Here is a never-to-be forgotten story. Carson Brown is the chairman of the John Volken Academy Advisory Committee in Arizona, and his wife, Jennifer, is also an advisory committee member. She is very politically involved and knows that John considers President Ronald Reagan one of his heroes. At a convention she attended in 2016, the keynote speaker was Ronald Reagan's personal adviser, Stephen Studdert. During Reagan's eight years in the White House, Studdert was by his side and Studdert continues to be a national leader in American public service.

At the conclusion of Studdert's speech, Jennifer felt compelled to share with him the story of a great admirer of Ronald Reagan, John Volken. He seemed keenly interested and asked her more questions about this man of whom he had never heard. He took off his cufflinks and held them in his hand, carefully showing the Presidential Seal on one side and the inscribed signature of President Reagan on the other. He explained that these were a personal gift from President Reagan, and that he wears them each time he speaks to remind him of the great man and the legacy he represents. He put them in Jennifer's hand and said, "I want you to give them to John. He deserves them more than I do."

Jennifer was certain that it would be more meaningful if Studdert himself gave John the cufflinks. However, with both men living outside of Arizona, scheduling a meeting of the two was nearly impossible. Months later, she arranged a dinner at the Sanctuary restaurant in Scottsdale AZ. Carson and Chawna were also in on the surprise.

When John was introduced to Studdert, tears welled up in his eyes. Studdert represented one of John's all time heroes—Ronald Reagan. Dinner was filled with lively discussions and laughs. During the conversation about the John Volken Academy, something miraculous happened. Carson casually mentioned that one of the graduates of the Academy was getting married the next day. He told the student's story and how he had always regretted not listening to advice from his mission president at the end of his two-year mission for his church. The inspired mission president had advised him to never touch prescription drugs under any circumstances. Ignoring this warning had set the young man on a path that led to years of heartache and regret. But thanks to the John Volken Academy, he had turned his life around. Studdert listened intently. He asked a few clarifying questions on the student's age and the area where he'd served as a missionary. And then he responded: "I don't believe in coincidences. I was his mission president."

No one at the table was aware that Studdert, after his time in the White House, had served in this volunteer capacity as mission president for the Church of Jesus Christ of Latter Day Saints, before his return to political public service. He remembered giving that warning to this young man. Carson immediately called the JVA graduate and handed Studdert the phone. They hadn't spoken since the young man left the mission. What a surprise; what a joy!

As the dinner continued, everyone absorbed the stories Studdert freely shared about President Reagan. He spoke of Reagan's determination to liberate East Germany and his part in successfully taking down the Berlin Wall. Studdert explained that on Airforce One to Germany, the speechwriters had twice removed the sentence, "Mr. Gorbachev, take down this wall." Twice, President Reagan put it back in, and the third time he didn't argue about it, and it didn't end up as part of the written speech. But while giving the speech, President Reagan added it back in and delivered it with such power that it's now his most famous quote. It was clear that Studdert was a part of the great work Reagan had done.

It was then that Studdert handed John the cufflinks.

John states, "I didn't anticipate anything special—just a dinner with friends. But the evening was much more than that. During the evening Studdert told many stories about Ronald Reagan. No wonder I admire him so much. What an exceptional man he was! We need him in our days."

"The 'party' was interrupted when the staff of the restaurant, very politely, urged us to leave. They kept the doors open longer just for us, but then they had to close. We continued our conversation outside."

John felt thrilled about the evening and honored to have Ronald Reagan's cufflinks. It was a never-to-be forgotten evening. "Thank you, Jennifer Brown."

CHAPTER 12

ANOTHER CHALLENGE

In early May 2008, John found himself with Bilhar Koonar, his long-time legal advisor—walking the rutted, sewage-filled lanes of Kibera, Africa's largest slum. Kibera lay six miles southeast of downtown Nairobi, Kenya, and was home to approximately 185,000 to over one million (no one knows for sure) desperately poor people who lived, typically, in 150-square-foot, tin-roofed shacks often housing eight people, mostly children. Large areas had no running water, few toilets, and little electricity. They were riddled with staggeringly high HIV/AIDS levels and orphan rates typical of other African cities inundated by the then-fatal disease. John was moved and overwhelmed by Kibera's poverty.

The Canadians' goal that day was to investigate the possibility of establishing an orphanage—with a linked school to help orphaned children learn independence and self-sufficiency. It was part of John's recent decision to take up a challenge made to him by Kenya's then-Foreign Minister, Marsden Madoka. The two men had met at an international conference of St. John Ambulance in Victoria, BC, the year before. St. John Ambulance is the world's oldest charity, dating back to the crusades in the eleventh, twelfth, and thirteenth centuries. Seated fortuitously beside each other, the two got talking and found they had a common interest. John heard about

Kenya's urgent needs, especially with the HIV/AIDS epidemic raging, and millions of Kenyan children losing their parents to the disease. When John explained that from the sale of his United Furniture business he'd set up the John Volken Foundation to do charitable work with needy people, Madoka said, "You have to come to Africa—you will make a difference."

The idea of establishing an African orphanage resonated with John. After all, at age nine he'd spent almost a year in an East German orphanage when his mother was ill. Regular meals, new friendships, and a sense of mischievous camaraderie with the other kids colored his memories favorably.

Almost a decade before his first trip to Kenya—during the years his furniture empire was rapidly expanding—John had considered finding a way to help orphans. Part of the impetus was based on his Christian principles of service. Doing good, paying tithing, volunteering, and being socially generous are all part of his convictions. Matthew 25:40[3] is often on his mind and always an inspiration. As well, ever since his East German childhood, John had an appreciative impression of orphanages and their positive effect of sparing children from the worst consequences of abandonment. He'd already launched his Welcome Home project in Vancouver, initially established to provide the city's often drug-addicted young street people with basic shelter and care.

Madoka met John and Bilhar Koonar at the Nairobi airport in 2008 and took them to his own rural village where a celebration marked their arrival. There was native drumming and dancing and welcoming greetings from local villagers—all very impressive to the Canadian visitors. But John felt a vague sense of disquiet because he realized the Foreign Minister was hoping John would fund an orphanage in his village, without John having had an opportunity to look at alternatives.

So, John and his entourage moved on, learning about the opportunities for supporting orphanages elsewhere, and more importantly, learning about the risks and legal constraints involved with building a big orphanage.

---

3 And the King shall answer and say unto them, "Inasmuch as ye have done it unto one of the least of these my brethren, ye have done it unto me."

While with Madoka checking out potential sites on a drive toward the Kenyan port of Mombasa, John got a first-hand lesson in the country's pervasive graft. Police stopped the vehicle and demanded a fifty-dollar bribe to let John travel farther, saying it was illegal for foreigners to travel at night. Madoka, seated in the vehicle's back, said nothing.

They asked, "Don't you know our laws? We can confiscate your car if you don't pay." John looked back. Madoka was smiling. He was not only one of the country's leading political figures, he was also a major in the Kenyan army.

Then Madoka stepped out of the car. The police officers realized immediately who they were trying to shake down. John watched in amusement as the officers' tone shifted from bullying to obsequious as they "Yes, sirred" and "No, sirred" Madoka.

But it was not simply this brief lesson in extortion but also cautionary information from other long-time foreign aid officials who warned John against doing any big-project development work in Kenya. Bribery, embezzlement, and theft were endemic. In addition, the laws in the country made it difficult for foreigners to acquire Kenyan lands; instead requiring foreign investors to work through local entities on aid projects. The vast Kenyan bureaucracy, John realized, meant that many fingers would touch the John Volken Foundation's monies required to get anything done.

Gabrielle Steed was John's assistant then. "At first he had a plan to build a large orphanage—like a Western-style building—with multiple floors, concrete, a school dormitory, etc. etc. Having been in Africa myself many times, I had seen abandoned projects everywhere because they weren't culturally appropriate. The funding agencies didn't consult with the local people. It ran well while the foreigners were in charge, but once they pulled out and left the locals in charge, things deteriorated fast. There was money, but no accountability, no monitoring reports, no effort to understand what was really needed."

In his consultation with local development officials during that trip, John learned that Steed's worries were well-founded. Koonar researched successful aid projects and the many that were unsuccessful, and they began to realize that the concept of a big orphanage was problematic.

People kept saying, "I hope you know what you're doing." They said, "First thing you do is put a big wall around any construction site because the contractor will deliver the lumber one day, and the next day the lumber will be gone. And if you hire somebody to do the work, by the time you're back in Canada, they and the money may likely be gone, too."

The architectural plans and designs of the large, Western style, Lift the Children orphanage were already drawn up and paid for. But when Madoka, who was always very supportive, introduced John and company to the manager of a typical African orphanage, she re-confirmed what they had heard. She convinced them that they should abandon their original plans, search out some of the thousands of existing needy orphanages, and support them instead.

Confronted with these realities, John followed this advice and searched for small, established orphanages across Kenya and Uganda. Orphanages with the most urgent needs that had the appropriate infrastructure and right management team were selected. This circumvented the possibility of bureaucratic red tape and graft and increased the chances that John Volken Foundation monies would reach some of the country's most needy 2.5 million orphans. Furthermore, contributing to locally run orphanages meant that local people, familiar with the issues, would have a direct say in a project's success. And the villagers or slumdwellers would, in turn, be lifted along with the orphans in their midst. The monthly budget from the John Volken Foundation was and still is $25,000 per month, plus donations.

As the ensuing months passed, John, his always supportive wife Chawna, and his friend Paul Christensen (and on one occasion his oldest daughter Lisanne who was then sixteen years old, and who loved Africa and the children) visited Kenya numerous times, continuing to look for established orphanages the Volken Foundation could support. John recalls:

> We visited scores of orphanages. All requested support, but many didn't require additional funding, so for one reason or another, we declined their request. During those visits I found it interesting to learn about the large

number of orphanages supported by Dutch people. What makes the Netherlands or its people so giving?

We selected ninety-two orphanages that we felt qualified for our support. Over the years, the numbers have been reduced to about sixty because of misuse of funds or because the orphanages became self-sufficient. Others closed down for health reasons.

One day, Minister Madoka and John drove along the border of the slum city of Kibera, when John suggested to Madoka, "Hey, let's go see."

Madoka responded with an emphatic, "No! You may never be seen again."

That didn't discourage John, and with Paul Christensen, who accompanied John on many of his trips to Africa, he visited Kibera at another time. He remembers: "No words can possibly describe the desperate conditions of that city within a city. One tin 'house' supported by the next, large areas without running water, electricity, or toilets . . . starving children . . . But the people were friendly and humble, although as visitors we received suspicious looks."

John was not deterred.

At Impersario Rehabilitation Centre in the slums of Kibera in May 2008, he met Peter Nyagesera, the founder and director of the facility, which housed dozens of orphans, ages seven to fourteen. Most had been illiterate when they'd been taken in and had survived by fending for themselves through petty crime, begging, or hawking fruit or snacks to motorists on Nairobi's crowded roads. The center was, like its children, destitute—with virtually no money. It was clearly in need of urgent assistance.

John and company visited the Gathaithi Orphanage and Vulnerable Children Centre, located on five acres of land about a ninety-minute drive north of Nairobi. The Gathaiti facility served kids ages four to fifteen, providing meals, shelter, clothing, and education for about 120 children.

They visited the Jehovah Jireh Children's Home, east of Nairobi, its facilities donated by a defunct mining company. There, forty-six orphaned children, ages nine to sixteen years old, got shelter, food, and an education.

They visited the Jenracy Children's Home in a shanty-town east of Nairobi. Consisting of six, corrugated-iron-sheet buildings, the facility was home to nineteen orphans, ages six to seventeen, who were sheltered, fed, and educated there. Thirty more local children were schooled there as well.

John was moved by the schools' and the surrounding slums' terrible poverty and by the determination of the dedicated individuals facing the challenges.

The more Kenyan orphanages John visited and the more he spoke with those running them, the more he understood the tremendous challenges. "So many orphanages, so much need. Above all, so many lonely, sick, hungry children." He tells of yet another experience during his Kenyan travels:

> One woman invited us into her house. She'd been a school teacher, and she saw all the kids on her street— no home, no nothing, stealing and starving. "So, I took them in," she said.
> I asked, "How do you support yourself?"
> "We don't have any permanent donors. But at night I go to certain restaurants that allow me to take their leftovers. We survive."
> "Do you always have enough food for the kids?"
> "Seldom; sometimes I come home with nothing."
> "Nothing? What do you tell the kids when there is nothing to eat?"
> "Well, we are all hungry, and I tell them, 'Maybe we'll eat tomorrow.' And the kids, quite satisfied, almost enthusiastically say, 'Yeah, maybe we'll eat tomorrow!'"

John, clearly struck by the poignancy of the comment and response, repeats thoughtfully, "Maybe we'll eat tomorrow. We in North America are so spoiled."

As experiences like these assaulted John, the urgency to do something propelled him into action.

His work in Kenya—and later in Uganda—has too often encountered roadblocks, conflicts, changed goals, unexpected realities, corruption of government, and disappointments with "friends." But turning to his abiding belief in change, he always finds a new route to pursue.

At the outset, John named his African orphanage Welcome Home for Children, echoing his Vancouver project's name. In time, Welcome Home for Children became Lift the Children (LTC), just as in Vancouver, guided by the effective suggestion of the advisory committee and students, Welcome Home became the John Volken Academy (JVA).

John's decision to change direction in Kenya—from building one large Nairobi facility to supporting scores of orphanages with the infrastructure already in place—came about from visiting the many orphanages scattered between Nairobi and Mombasa, Kenya's second-largest city, and Uganda. Each time he stopped, he heard how grateful the operators would be for him to help them financially. He recalls one conversation with a man at an orphanage that went like this:

"We barely get enough food for the children. The water is cut off. What we really need is water, and money to pay for electricity."

John asked, "How much would that cost?"

"Just a few dollars a month."

John committed to support this orphanage. Then he asked the man if he lived with the children in the orphanage, to which he replied that he didn't; he lived quite far away. So, John asked, "Do you have a car?"

The man laughed and said, "I don't even have a bicycle."

"I felt insensitive," says John, amused now at his naïveté. "I should have known . . . "

To administer the LTC program, a thirty-one-year-old Kenyan law student named Emmanuel was interviewed and hired. He'd grown up in a Nairobi slum, one of three children of a destitute and uneducated mother. When he was a child, food had been scarce, money for school fees frequently unavailable, and his mother's begging on street corners was often unavoidable. Many of his young friends had turned to drugs or crime to survive. But Emmanuel, determined to escape this situation, managed to finish high school and avoid the temptations inherent in urban poverty in Africa. It was through being a member of The Church of Jesus Christ of Latter-day Saints that he got financial assistance to attend university. And it was through these same connections that he got to meet John, who was at the time looking for someone to manage the growing LTC orphanage initiative.

"It's really quite difficult for someone who doesn't know the place to operate in Kenya," says Emmanuel. "Different people. Different backgrounds. Different expectations. Different culture. Trust issues are challenging. Especially if you have money. Money is often wasted. In fact, it can easily disappear. You probably need to get someone on the ground who really understands and is willing to share your visions, who's willing to make an impact."

The more John heard, the more he sensed Emmanuel's commitment to the LTC program. He hired him to be its field director. Emmanuel, in conjunction with his LTC advisors, gradually began implementing systems for the regular monitoring of Lift the Children orphanages. They insisted that standards must be met, and bookkeeping must occur, eliminating those who were not fulfilling their contractual obligations, while fostering connections that would benefit all LTC facilities. Some orphanages now have large gardens, producing food for the children and for profit. Some are linked to neighborhood businesses for job training and free supplies. Some have developed food-collection networks, bringing in local restaurants' leftovers. Some work cooperatively, sharing food, curriculum ideas, business connections, micro-financing opportunities, and staff. Others have set up attached schools for educational outreach to parented children and local adults.

On a visit with John at his Surrey office in Canada during the spring of 2017, Emmanuel accounted for his work with Lift the Children. Before he was hired, the LTC had a policy of locating needy Kenyan orphanages and providing varying amounts of financial support based on the number of children in the facility. The more children there and the greater the need, the more money that was given. There was little oversight on how the money was actually spent. Not surprisingly, some of those running the orphanages would simply collect street children—upping their facility's population—but providing little care or education. Once he began looking at the funding system, Emmanuel realized the financing was, in some cases, being misused. It was, he knew, a commonplace African situation where generous Western donors were uncertain and lax toward fiscal accountability.

John knew from his own experience that people have the capacity to change, to better themselves, and, as a consequence, better the world.

He wanted Lift the Children to operate on this principle. Emmanuel explains:

My job is to make sure the funds are used the best way possible. You don't want to just put money somewhere. Children need to have a roof and food. Good learning with an empty stomach is challenging. But it's not really changing their lives. They need to be able to read. They need to have life skills and job skills. They need a sense of purpose. If you give them a fish you feed them for a day, if you teach them how to fish you feed them for life.

A lot of multinational non-profits just give money. That's why things in Africa haven't changed much. Their money just produces more dependency. All too often, the non-profits never think about how to sustain change, how to free people from the cycle of poverty and dependence.

There's an old African saying: You can take a man from the village, but it's difficult to remove the village from him. Or, if you can change a man's perceptions about himself and his possibilities, it's easy for him to change. That's self-sustainability. That's the model of Lift the Children. You change your perceptions, so you can change your situation. At Lift the Children, we want to help people help themselves. We don't want to create a syndrome where you give money, and it just becomes a tool for consumption. We are not really helping if people are just consuming, and never thinking, *What can I do to become self-reliant?*

Part of Emmanuel's job is to instill in the staff of the Lift the Children orphanages the principles of budgeting, planning, setting realistic goals, and applying good teaching techniques. LTC workshops are held where people are trained in small-business management and classroom skills. Where there are adjacent areas of fertile soil, the LTC will bring in authorities to talk about sustainable agriculture. Then, the teachers and the children get directly involved: designing, planting, and later harvesting produce from these new gardens.

In practical terms, LTC provides thirty to sixty percent of its orphanages' total financial support. The orphanages determine how the money is spent: typically, twenty percent for food; fifty percent on rental of buildings; and thirty percent on staff salaries. Emergencies, sudden medical costs, school supplies, and uniforms often eat into these proportions. Lift the Children requires that the orphanages raise the remaining seventy percent of their overall costs from other, often local, sources. Says Emmanuel, "We encourage those running the orphanages to seek alternative resources. For example, they can appeal to farmers, who can donate vegetables to the orphanage, or appeal to companies that produce food, such as bakeries, that can donate surplus bread. Some of the orphanages have schools. Some of them have turned them into income-generating sources—as kids from the local community pay school fees. One orphanage has a sustainable permaculture farm the LTC helped establish. They make $1,200 a month selling their produce."

Emmanuel admits that, although support is often promised before each federal election, Kenyan government officials do very little for the country's countless orphans. Kenya, a country of 48 million faces the multiple dangers produced by extreme drought—and occasional terrorism—in the northeast; the flight of millions of rural farmers and herders to the urban slums of Nairobi and Mombasa; an ongoing HIV/AIDS epidemic; an ever-growing population of orphans; and an unemployment rate of almost twenty percent.

From John's perspective, his trips to Kenya proved to be eye-opening and profound. Nothing, not even the worst circumstances of post-war East Germany, had prepared him for what he encountered there. In East Germany, there'd been times of scarcity and hunger, but not the Nairobi slums' smells of open defecation and the obvious dangers of diarrhea. Not the tropical heat and muddy lanes and rudimentary shacks, packed together by the tens of thousands—without running water or electricity or toilets. He was often struck with the realization that, even in these perilous circumstances, he could find evidence of fortitude. In the orphanages, the children seemed happy, taking comfort from the security and nutrition and social interactions the places provided. They'd gather around John, looking up at the white visitors, who were somewhat of a novelty.

"I get chills just thinking about it," says John, turning the pages of his photo albums covering his African travels. "We were at this Catholic orphanage," he continues, pointing at the pictures, "the kids all jumping around, happy, noisy. And there's this little boy just looking at me, staring at me, saying nothing. So, I said, 'How are you doing?' He just kept on looking at me. I felt like he wanted me to do something. So, I said, 'Come here,' and picked him up, holding him. He just kept staring at me. I tickled him. No response. A nun standing close by told me the boy's name was . . . I think it was Danny. She asked him, 'Do you want to go home with John?' He never said anything, but enthusiastically nodded his head. When we finally had to leave, I tried to put him down. That little boy, with a frightened face, was holding onto me tighter. So, I gently forced him to get down, and we walked toward our mini-bus. I took his hand as we walked. (That's when the photo was taken, which is now part of the Lift the Children Logo.) When I got on the bus, he began to cry. It broke my heart! Even now, I get teary, remembering the incident. He never said a word to me."

John studies the photo for a while and, regaining his composure, finally says, "I wonder what happened to him. There are so many heartbreaking stories . . . "

On his last two journeys to Kenya, John joined Emmanuel as they travelled amid the urban orphanages of Nairobi and Mombasa, and the rural ones that lie between the two cities. They talked about management and accountability and the principles of sustainability that underpinned how the Lift the Children orphanages worked. Emmanuel explained how LTC orphanage personnel would go looking for young children, often homeless and starving amid the cities' sprawling slums. Some were as young as three years old. Everyone knew that if they were left on the street and survived, the children would, almost inevitably, become involved with crime. Some would be murdered. Others would get HIV/AIDS and spread the disease. Still others would get addicted to drugs and waste their lives. Some of the street kids had mothers or fathers who'd abandoned them. Some were literally lost and didn't know who their parents were or where they lived. Many of the kids had been sexually abused.

John saw the conditions in Kenya's shantytowns and streets and orphanages, and it seemed to Emmanuel that he found the realities almost overwhelming. "Sometimes he'd shed tears just through the interactions he had with the children," Emmanuel says. "I think what also made him so emotional is he'd look at the kids and their situation and try to compare it to where he'd come from and what he'd experienced previously. That really made him sad. I'm pretty sure he couldn't believe people were living in such circumstances at this point in time—the twenty-first century. In the shantytowns . . . kids trying to survive, no father, no mother, some of them without shoes or food. You see the situation they're living in. The humblest of situations. Many of the kids, all they can afford to give is a smile. John would see this, and it affected him deeply."

John tells the story about his visit to the Missionary of the Poor in Kampala, Uganda:

> There I witnessed the misery and challenges of this world; the most severely mentally and physically handicapped of Africa were being lovingly nursed by volunteers. Most of the population couldn't move without help. Some were dying. Six men were standing tied against the wall, secured with strings. They were literally just skin and bones and couldn't stand on their own. They had been carried outside for a short time to enjoy a little sun. The eyes of those helpless individuals were blank, staring, yet I saw something that seemed to say, *I am grateful. I am okay.* Many of the caregivers, or monks as they call themselves, were holding the hands of the needy, feeding or washing them, just trying to make them comfortable in any way they could. Some of the young men were washing diapers

in a long cement trough with running water—diapers, not of children. The only ones who could walk were the dozen or so albinos. These unfortunates were living in constant fear for their lives because many Africans believe that good fortune comes their way if a body part from an albino is buried in the foundation of their house. Some Africans are satisfied with a body part from a "perfect specimen"—the reason why many parents maim their children to keep them safe.

I realize that words cannot bring the experience alive. However, it is branded in my heart and in my brain and when I hear people complain, "Poor me," I often think to myself, *Really*?!

One evening, before dinner, I had the opportunity to spend some time with one of these young volunteers. During the conversation I wanted to know what had inspired him to do what he did, so I started with, "For how long will you do this?"

"For the rest of my life. I am committed to do the work. I am grateful to be able to do this."

"So, you are never going on a date or experience the love of a woman?"

"It doesn't even compare with the love we experience here . . ."

"So, you'll never experience family or your own children?"

"This is my family and my children."

And finally, I asked, "Why do you do this?"

"This is what Jesus would do."

Those were pretty well the exact words spoken. This was one of those unforgettable moments. It pierced my heart. I felt it. It was true: *This is what Jesus would do*. It humbled me with the compelling thought to be more Christ-like. That was only the beginning of an impactful evening . . . There, dressed in white, in a long hall alongside two rows of tables, were these special young men, about sixty of them, standing and singing hymns. One title, "Hum

Hum," may not be especially inspiring, but that hymn (or perhaps it was the day's experience) had a profound spiritual/emotional impact on me. At the end, I was in tears and that is when the leader asked me to say the blessing on the food. Everyone in the hall was very patient as it took me at least thirty long seconds before I had my emotions under control and could utter the blessing . . . It was one of the most spiritual and memorable days of my life.

I am grateful that my wife Chawna and my daughter Lisanne could witness the occasion. To say it was special is an understatement. We visited the Missionary of the Poor several times and sent them a container of needed material—wheelbarrows, bicycles, shovels, bedding, clothing, food, etc."

Africa! I found that Africa has the worst and the best people, the most giving and the most selfish. Much of the strife among them may be blamed on the Europeans when they divided the countries by straight borders, never taking the different tribes into consideration. Kenya is still very tribal—and the bloodshed during elections is evidence of that. Politicians are in many ways still the tribal leaders to be obeyed. Sadly, they are often corrupt. However, the general population is humble and trying to survive the best they can.

We met many who had nothing, yet gave . . . What an example to all of us.

On one wall in the "Africa Room," a meeting room located just down the hall from John's office in Surrey, are sixty framed photographs. Taken during his Africa trips, they show some of the orphanages Lift the Children supports—and the faces of hundreds of children looking outward with expressions of happiness and hope.

The John Volken Foundation (not Academy) contributes $300,000 per year to the African endeavor, plus money raised by volunteers in support of the orphanages in Uganda and Kenya. Lift the Children has no paid employees, except for three wage earners in Africa, whose salaries are paid for by donations.

Unfortunately, John fell seriously ill during his last visit and came to the realization that his travels amid Kenyan and Ugandan slums and rural villages presented too much of a health risk to continue. He has now left the daily running of the projects in Africa to Zachuas Ogonji. Emmanuel has been accepted to Brigham Young University in Utah to study law. But John constantly reminds those on the advisory committee in Canada and otherwise involved to make every dollar count and help the children realize the opportunity to rise above their circumstances—with the end goal of being self-sufficient and **walking with a purpose.**

Lift the Children

Faces of Africa...

...with Chawna, my daughter Lisanne and Kenya's foreign Minister Marsden Madoka (MM)

CHAPTER 13

THE JOHN VOLKEN ACADEMY PROGRAM
It's Not Easy, but It's Worth It

Our Mission

TO BE A WORLD LEADER IN

PROVIDING

THE MOST EFFECTIVE AND AFFORDABLE
RESIDENTIAL ADDICTION TREATMENT

CULTIVATING

SELF-WORTH AND STRONG CHARACTER

TEACHING

LEADERSHIP AND PRACTICAL JOB SKILLS

ADVANCING

SECONDARY AND POST-SECONDARY EDUCATION

INSTILLING

IN EACH STUDENT THE DETERMINATION
TO BE THE BEST THAT THEY CAN BE
FOR THEMSELVES,
FOR THEIR FAMILIES,
AND FOR THEIR COMMUNITY.

Our Core Values

We believe in God and in being obedient
to the law and subject to authorities.

We uphold the dignity of each individual.

We believe in humility, forgiveness,
accountability, determination, work,
learning, service, and responsibility.

Daily, before breakfast, dinner, and on special occasions, students recite this PROMISE with power and emphasis like a cadence, while standing, bold and proud.

MY PROMISE

My life was out of control. My addiction was controlling me.
I had the choice to continue on my path of self-destruction
or change and rebuild my life.
I chose to change.
The John Volken Academy provides all the tools I need to change
and as brothers and sisters we help each other in this struggle.

However

I alone am responsible for achieving my full potential.

I'm changing my attitude.
I'm changing my behavior.
I'm changing my values.
I am changing my life!
The power to succeed lies within me.

I will graduate from the John Volken Academy
and be the best person I can be—
for myself, for my family, and for my community.

This I promise.

The John Volken Academy curriculum addresses all areas of development. Every student is expected to exert themselves to progress on the following principles:

- To be positive, motivating, forgiving, unselfish, open-minded, tolerant, reliable, friendly, honest, trustworthy

- To communicate effectively and cooperate with others

- To be responsible, accountable, and respectful

- To develop patience, tolerance, and perseverance

- To develop humility, self-control, and excellence in standards

- To improve self-confidence and deal with changes and criticism

- To learn management and leadership skills and problem solving

- To learn business principles and entrepreneurship

- To be valuable employees and take pride in performance

- To deal with the public, consequences, opposition, and criticism

- To be givers instead of takers and go the extra mile

- To be punctual, polite, reliable, and productive

- To enjoy a wide range of indoor and outdoor activities without the use of any stimulants

- To learn manners and etiquette

- To enjoy the arts, museums, operas, plays, and recitals

- To pursue advanced education, extensive career training, and attend workshops and stimulating lessons

- Above all, John Volken Academy students develop their characters and a healthy lifestyle on the way to becoming the best that they can be.

John says of the demanding curriculum:

Many individuals that come into the program have done four, five, even up to twelve short-term programs previously and realize that a short-term program simply isn't enough. More time is required for their brains to heal and for them to adopt a new, healthy lifestyle—and all time is structured. The mantra at the John Volken Academy is for students to be busy 24/7. When they're sleeping, they're busy sleeping. When they're eating, they're busy eating. When they're pursuing their responsibilities, they learn to be good employees. During activity times, they have fun, and they learn social skills and team building.

There are evenings with experts on issues related to addiction and recovery; and evenings of games, educational videos, volunteering, or a walk in the park. There's a gym block for volleyball or exercise; there are times for reading or learning academics, or for special presentations—the list is endless. The focus is for students to become well-rounded individuals.

The JVA is not faith-based; however, spiritual development is very much encouraged. It makes no difference in the recovery process what religion a student believes in, or, for that matter, does not believe in. However, a major help in the quest for sobriety is when a student goes on his or her knees and prays for strength—at the least it is self-fulfilling. Grace is said before each meal and on all appropriate occasions. On Sundays, students are encouraged to attend church services of their choice. While religious or spiritual leaders are welcomed by management and students alike, there is no proselyting. The only purpose of the John Volken Academy is to help individuals embrace life-long sobriety and continue on their way to become the best that they can be.

The day starts at 6:00 a.m. That is when the alarms go off every morning at the dormitories of the John Volken Academy in Surrey, BC, and Kent, WA. On the ranch in Arizona, students get up at 5:00 a.m., and during the summertime at 4:00 a.m. The 40º-plus Celsius/110º-plus Fahrenheit heat during the summer makes it necessary. Some get up before regular wake-up time to jog or exercise. There's little time to be pussyfooting. Showering, brushing their teeth, making their beds with military precision, cleaning the bedroom and making it tidy—all this needs to be done to be ready for breakfast at 5:15 or 6:30 a.m. Food is served cafeteria-style, prepared by students who have been up since well before dawn. Breakfasts, like all meals, are healthy, tasty, well-balanced, plentiful, and different every day. One cup of coffee is permitted each morning—the only stimulant the students are allowed during their stay at the JVA. Before acceptance into the John Volken Academy Program, students must commit to being weaned off any addictive substances.

After breakfast, the students meet with a senior student or program director to schedule their responsibilities for that day. Before their daily responsibilities begin, there is an hour of student group-work on emotional, personal, and interpersonal issues aimed at promoting reflection on the students' progress. Depending on the day, the weather, or the location, there's an hour of exercise. Physical fitness is an integral part of the program, and each location is provided with extensive exercise equipment. Then students begin their daily responsibilities, which vary depending on location. Late afternoon and evening are busy with learning or mind-challenging activities. Second-year students spend about ten hours a week on book learning or in other educational and career-linked activities. At 10:00 p.m. each weekday, it's quiet time, for reading, writing, or other quiet activities. At 11:00 p.m. lights are out.

At the beginning, the program requires little of a student and accelerates with time. It starts with learning to **walk purposefully**, no hands in pockets, no slouching or leaning. Then, gradually, it moves to learning how to deal with future disappointment or rejection. For example, a young man leaves the program, meets a girl, and thinks he is in love. If she rejects him, it could lead to relapse. If he gets the perfect job and gets laid off—relapse. He loses a finger in an accident—relapse. Somebody's unfair to him—relapse. At the John Volken Academy, students learn how to handle these challenges by being somewhat "bombarded" with unpleasant situations all day long. One pivotal factor in this is the "Pull-Up." At the least indication of failure to follow the JVA student manual, an observing student will call out the "offending student" by name with, "Check yourself." Then the observing student will explain what's wrong or offensive. The student being pulled-up can only respond with, "Thank you." He cannot argue. He must listen . . . and reflect. Students are required, in this way, to control their impulsive reactions while learning to handle the "triggers" and change their behavior. That can be frustrating. But the bi-weekly, two-hour Encounter Groups, facilitated by experienced group leaders, are there to relieve their frustrations. It is all designed to handle challenges in a safe place without the drugs and alcohol.

Condoning is viewed as a serious negative behavior. Most students have historical patterns of secrecy and lying, "turning a blind eye." The number-one street code of "don't snitch or tell" reinforces this negative behavior and contributes to guilt while it is toxic to the community and keeps people ill. This must never be tolerated.

Given the students' multiple addictions, their years of lying and deception, their often fractured family dynamics, and their propensity toward short-term thinking, it's not surprising that, despite all efforts, infractions against the JVA's rules and a desire to quit the program occur and are expected.

John laughs ironically when he says, "Sometimes I feel like a stern headmaster, handing out punishments, although the word 'punishment' is a no-no. Instead, we use the term 'learning experience.' But if we don't have consequences in place—and apply them—there would be no consequential thinking."

There's "The Bench." Every student knows they go to The Bench to sit and reflect when they are out of control in their thinking or actions. People at the academy know the pressures that come with changing. The Bench is a place for people to sit and think about consequences, instead of just saying, "Okay, I'm out of here," and leaving. That knee-jerk impulsiveness is how people end up with a needle in their arm.

John sums up the sad facts about many of the origins of drug addiction:

A young man or woman laments to a doctor, "I'm so depressed." And he or she receives the response, "Here's an anti-depressant." This can be the first step towards hell. They're often good kids. Maybe smart . . . with straight A's. Maybe they suffered a sports injury and needed painkillers. The prescription drug makes them feel good. I've heard it over and over. Legally prescribed pharmaceuticals—like Valium and OxyContin—often become the gateway to misery. And while doctors may mean well, they are often a major cause of drug addiction. People get hooked on those anti-depressants or painkillers. Then they start sharing prescription drugs with their friends. And drinking. Smoking. Soon "advancing" to crack cocaine, heroin . . . the choices seem endless.

Over time, the brain actually changes, and the addiction becomes a disease . . . a chronic disease. Now, even if they want to quit, they can't, unless they get help. Some of them go through a dozen or even more short-term treatments without success. They try self-medicating, but that doesn't work either.

The secret is, "One day at a time." Students characteristically "rush" their recovery. They underestimate the time it takes to change, and they overestimate the progress they have made. Putting the emphasis on living right each hour and each day reduces anxiety, while impatience with the duration of recovery often leads to premature dropout and relapse.

If any unsettling behaviors continue for the wayward student—and they often do—it's certain they'll become the focus of one of John's "My Challenge Nights." The focus on changing is relentless.

Once a month in Surrey, Kent, and Gilbert, John leads the "Challenge Night" with all students present. He singles out the students with more serious challenges. Describing this, John momentarily role-plays both sides of "poking the bear." He usually starts out with naming the student and asks, "How are you doing?"

"I'm okay."

"If you are okay, then why are you here?"

"Oh, I guess I've got problems."

"Problems? That would be a problem. The good news is you have no problems—you have challenges. Do you know the difference? Challenges are to be overcome; they help us to grow. It takes courage, trust, commitment, humility—you can learn to overcome challenges. Problems, however, can be much more difficult to handle. To successfully deal with problems, that is a challenge. Does that make sense?"

While the student thoughtfully nods his head, John delves into it. "Tell me your issues. What are your challenges? What's behind that? What are you angry at? What makes you feel that way? How do you think you can fix that? Tell me about your feelings, your anger, your frustrations." He pokes them with questions and makes observations. They have to come clean. *Absolute honesty is fundamental in your recovery. Secrets keep you sick* is one of the program's principles. John feels that parents are often too judgmental. "We're not. All students have 'similar issues,' however, each one is unique. It is important that they understand the meaning of forgiveness."

Any kind of forgiveness is hard, but fundamental for true recovery. Like love, forgiveness never stays the same, never ends, but deepens over the years.

"When I have exhausted my deliberation with that particular student," John continues, "I invite all students to express their feelings and opinions. They open up and see their own faults in others. These sessions are often emotional; you might even say they are 'sacred happenings.' There are tears. It is healing—it is life changing."

During their time in active addiction, most students don't understand the long-term effects of drug use. The brain doesn't mature until the mid-twenties and generally, emotional maturity is impeded and stunted when a person becomes addicted. The fact that youthful drug use has stunted their maturity is a challenge to deal with. You get twenty-four-year-olds with a sixteen-year-old's emotional state or mentality. They're impatient. They think, *Two or three weeks, maybe,* or *I'm all better now.* The fact is, they are sober, yes. But they are still the very same addicts. Prolonged use of drugs and alcohol affects the brain. If a student leaves the program too soon, they often relapse. Almost guaranteed. That's the problem with most short-term programs. Out the door and right back to the drugs. It takes a long-term program to allow the brain the needed time to heal and to adopt a new lifestyle.

That is the compelling reason why the JVA is a minimum two-year, and up to five-year, program. It takes the brain up to five years to get to the point of maximum healing.

Healing and changing while in recovery requires active participation. There is no magic pill. Changing long-held behaviors, attitudes, and self-image involves struggling and even suffering. Developing physical strength, stamina, and endurance requires commitment, focus, effort, discipline, sacrifice, hard work, and sometimes boring practice. But mainly it involves aches, pain, and sometimes the fear associated with stretching beyond previous limits. There is no gain without pain.

Once students have reached the fourth stage of the program, typically toward the end of their first year, the JVA's education coordinator in each facility begins interviewing them to assess their academic needs and career plans.

Dr. Brad Barrett jump-started and developed the education program of the John Volken Academy. He is well qualified, with a doctoral degree in education. He was the superintendent for the Gilbert School District for decades, and still teaches at a university level. He regularly visits with the students, often for hours at a time, tutoring them to help them obtain their GED, helping them prepare for their university entrance exam, counseling them regarding special career requirements, or even mentoring them on how to achieve their bachelor's degree. He is a member of the John Volken Academy Advisory Committee in Phoenix and tirelessly advances the education program at all three John Volken Academy facilities. He plays an integral role in helping students to become the best that they can be.

Some of the students have used drugs from the time that they were as young as twelve years old. They don't really know themselves. They don't know their strengths or sometimes even their interests. The education coordinator conducts an aptitude test and helps them every step of the way on their educational journey.

With all this done, the program allows ten hours a week for advanced book learning, and for that the students are given access to the computer lab for their online studies. During this period, the students are motivated and begin seeing their futures more clearly, leaving their pasts behind.

They study online for graphic design, computer science, sustainable agriculture, aromatherapy, auto mechanics, fitness training, real estate, Spanish, psychology, nursing, business, accounting, and engineering. Acquiring one's high school diploma is a fundamental requirement for graduation.

To add to the curriculum, volunteers and many advisory committee members regularly come to the academy to provide workshops, tutoring, and general support.

Anecdotal scenes and actions with John in the Surrey academy (and similarly in Gilbert, AZ and Kent, WA), look and sound like this:

Scene One: He opens doors, chats with students, and shows a visitor the various places where the young men and women take classes, undergo therapy, study, play basketball, lift weights, eat, and socialize. In the computer room, several students are working at online high school or university courses aimed at getting a diploma or a job-related certificate to prepare for a future beyond the academy. Heads turn momentarily, greetings and smiles are exchanged, and the students continue their studies.

Scene Two: In the large, modern cafeteria, a half-dozen students stand behind the kitchen counter, ready to serve lunch to the sixty or so students. A student leader welcomes guests and any new students, followed by applause. Then the young men and women stand and repeat "The Promise" in a cadence. "The Promise" is John's creation, and he says it took him on and off about a year to write it, constantly changing it. It wasn't one of his priorities. Now it is repeated before breakfast and dinner—a recurring assertion of their commitment to the guiding principles of the John Volken Academy. After that, a senior student asks a student to bless the food. Upon finishing the blessing, table by table, the students carry their plates to the kitchen counter and are served by their peers, who have prepared the food as part of their ongoing training as potential restaurant cooks and chefs. Seated again around the table, while enjoying the meal, the students engage in light conversation, including "Word of the Day," where each student has the choice of forming a sentence that includes at least two of the six words given. Some students want to cram all six words into one sentence. "It is fun and challenging at the same time. It promotes thinking." There is laughter or more serious discussion about the challenges of changing their lives.

The young men and women agree it's often a struggle. Says one, "I'm just one bad decision away from being back on the street." The young men shake their heads at the idea of leaving, however tempting they admit it is at times, especially during the critical first few months. Of one student who left a few days ago another student says, "I heard he overdosed." Yeah—silence.

"This is the reality one never gets used to," John admits.

Absolute honesty is fundamental to recovery. Secrets keep you sick.

The ability to trust others is very important to personal and emotional growth and never more so than when individuals are expected to behave as they should, rather than as they have been.

Do it right and you will understand why you have been doing it wrong.

You cannot continue what you have been doing and expect different results. It is not just an exercise in conformity, but an essential tool for making a complete change.

Feelings, insights, and altered self-perception often follow (rather than precede) behavior change.

Scene Three: Behind the training store in Surrey is a buffer zone between commercial properties and residential. It's a "green" area where early in the morning John indulges in his lifelong love of gardening or enjoys the garden next to the men's dorm lined with the cobble-lined creek that flows into a garden pool. And John—accompanied by a student, stoops and pulls weeds. Whatever needs doing, John is part of the solution or else he teaches it. "Hands on" was always very much a part of him and is well-known at the John Volken Academy.

Whenever you see something wrong, be instrumental in making it right. Be part of the solution.

Scene Four: Seated at the regular JVA Council meeting, John works his way through a lengthy thirty-item agenda. Around the boardroom table are JVA staff, including Chawna, plus the student president and his three counsellors. The purpose is to administer and improve the program and train staff and students.

The topics are many and varied, and discussions are to the point. Decisions are made, and items are gradually checked off. For example: There's an upcoming Scotia Bank marathon: "Who's going?" John asks. There are questions about phone usage—both incoming and outgoing—and whether students and parents should be allowed to talk at the time of a crisis. Animated and contrary opinions are aired. The JVA student president is looking for some help on Sunday—volunteers? The next graduation is coming in three weeks and invitations need to be written and sent out—anyone? And so it goes. John generally assumes a strong stance regarding rules being followed. Rules are meant to be adhered to. "This is not a vacation resort, but a change-your-life program," he admonishes.

Scene Five: In the PricePro warehouse, there's a discussion about what to do with a recent, huge delivery of overripe bananas. There are jokes about a near-future diet of banana bread. John is not amused. He'll have words with the wholesaler. In the JVA park sit a half-dozen students, chatting, playing guitar, or absorbing summer sunlight. To a visitor, it looks idyllic. It is difficult to imagine that these young men and women were once consumed by various entrenched addictions.

Scene Six: Once a month on Sunday nights and in his travel to Kent, WA, and Gilbert, AZ, there's an evening called "Message for Life," when John explores important practical or ethical themes like humility, wisdom, accountability, service, controlling one's thoughts, gratitude, determination, courage . . . the ever-so-important topic of forgiveness—and other inspiring subjects.

"Life is not meant to be easy or even fair," John teaches. "It's not what happens to you, but how you deal with it that matters. Attitude! We must train our thoughts and language to be positive and motivating, regardless of how down we may feel at the moment. You can look down and feel sorry for yourself, resulting in more negativity, or you can look up and be positive. Practice it and you will become more positive. It is your choice. The universe will reward the positive person. You will be healthier, have more friends, and live longer. Challenge yourselves to think about what you can learn from any experience, positive or negative . . . and if nothing comes to mind, there is always, 'I'll get through this and it will make me stronger.' But it's going to take willpower." And with that, he launches into the evening's topic: Willpower.

Students read short stories about willpower and comment on them. Then they are given a list of forty-one inspirational quotes and sayings on the topic. Every student reads one and John asks the students to reflect and comment on the meaning of these bits of wisdom as they apply them to themselves. Here are a few:

Will is character in action.
Great souls have wills; others have wishes.
Someday is not a day of the week.
The only good luck great men have is the determination to overcome bad luck.
Awareness by itself is not enough; it must be joined by mastery.
A thousand-mile journey begins with the first step.
Success is a ladder you cannot climb with your hands in your pockets.
The greatest waste in the world is the difference between what we are and what we could become.
Failure? I never encountered it. All I ever met were temporary setbacks.
And so on.

About two hours pass as the various aspects of willpower are discussed. Emphasis is on the will to get sober, stay sober, and become the best you can be. There are other serious thoughts but also light-hearted comments and laughter. It is all about learning, changing, and bonding.

John always ends the evening with encouraging words to his students. "Before you go to bed tonight, you do what?" and the students respond with: "Look in the mirror and convince the person in the mirror I am all right." John adds, "Let your subconscious mind work on it. You heard often enough: 'You are no good.' They were wrong, even irresponsible and—you must defeat that thought. You can, because you are doing all you can to become the best person you can be." John loves those evenings with his students—and so do they.

Remembering the pains and challenges of the past helps students stay committed to the struggle in the present and the goal of the future. Recovery is ongoing. It is important to acknowledge the past, but most important to put the past behind you. Do not dwell on it.

In Surrey, John is at home. He appears and disappears throughout the day in his administrative and instructional capacities at the academy. This is far less true during his three-to-six-day visits to the Washington, California, and Arizona academies where time limitations propel him through a whirlwind of meetings and student interactions. In Surrey, the minute-to-minute dealings with JVA students falls to the three program directors, Chris, Darren, and Landon, along with the student council president and other senior students. The former three are all graduates of the John Volken Academy. The addictions they deal with are varied: prescription and illegal drugs, alcohol, gambling, internet-use, sex, pornography, and eating disorders. They understand the challenges and the enormous difficulties every student faces.

From their vantage point, they are seldom surprised by what happens to students in their passage through the JVA program. Their responsibility is to be the rational authority to teach a healthy new lifestyle and motivate students to become the best that they can be.

Here is what happens from the time of intake to graduation:

For the first month, a new student—called an inductee—is isolated from everyone other than his fellow JVA students. There's no contact with any outside person, even friends or family. Only the minimal necessities are provided, and they are given simple maintenance responsibilities. They receive a personal seventeen-page student manual, containing the general outline from beginning to graduation, which they are required to study. As well, each inductee is assigned a "shadow," a more senior student who acts as a guide and friend during the first month. This shadow helps a new student through the initial stressful times. Yes, it is stressful.

"Wow! I'm here. I've got all this time ahead of me. Two years!" The inductee looks around and starts to compare himself with people who have two or three months left, and thinks, *I didn't say goodbye to Uncle Jerry. Or, I wonder how my dog Wolf is doing. Or, is my girlfriend going to wait for me?* Or whatever. All these reasons to use the phone, all these reasons to feel hopeless, all these reasons not to be here.

"Most students have doubts when they first get here," says John. "Many went through several programs before or tried to do it on their own. Nothing worked. This is their last chance. I emphasize that the John Volken Academy is not a two-year program, but it is a 'change-your-life program.' Two years sounds like jail. However, when you concentrate on your recovery, time flies, while it gives the brain the needed time to heal itself. All along you learn job skills, social skills, and life skills. And you adjust your emotional state and develop strong character—all needed for lifelong sobriety."

After the initial inductee period and after passing the freshman test, which is based on the student manual, comes the freshman period. Now more is expected from the students.

Step by step. In their aim to want things quickly, students often miss important steps in their learning. What is learned at one point becomes the foundation for the next piece of learning. The maxim is to focus on one thing at a time.

At each step along the way, the John Volken Academy Council meets to discuss the advancement of each student. How are they doing? Does someone need extra support or counseling? Are they ready for the next step? Why not? A monthly progress report is filled out after a thorough one-on-one interview each student has with a program director.

Each student is required to write a freshman letter describing the most destructive point of his or her addiction. The purpose of the letter is to face the worst emotions stirred up by those memories.

The tears flow, and they start to confess, "I've held this pain, I've locked this pain inside me . . . or pushed it down with drugs and alcohol for all these years."

John responds with, "Hey, it's okay to cry. Tears show that you feel and care."

That's often a major turning point for new students—crying. They feel emotions they never felt before. Drugs suppressed these feelings. Tears help to wash them away. The freshman letter is read aloud and then destroyed, signaling that it is time to move on.

"New" emotions or feelings are part of the healing process. Some students cry for the first time in years. These feelings were numbed out during active addiction, and because they are difficult to deal with, students often interpret them as negative. They think their healing process has stopped and that they are going backwards. The fact is they are making progress in their recovery and are feeling emotions and getting impressions that are signs of healing.

During the next period in the program, the junior period, students concentrate on learning to be model employees or future entrepreneurs. To demonstrate one's growth in awareness, each junior student is required to write a letter to those most adversely affected by the student's addiction, asking them what they went through and to write a letter about their ordeal. Again, it is read to the whole JVA community—again, there are welcomed tears of remorse. The letter is destroyed during a special burning celebration, signaling that that period in the students' lives is over. It is emotional and liberating!

During the fourth stage, the teacher period, the students are expected to take on more leadership roles with less responsibility in the day-to-day operations, while they advance their schooling and academic studies.

That period is followed by the seven-month re-entry period. Now students are trusted with furloughs. This time provides opportunities, to look for work, join alcohol and drug-support groups, volunteer, and complete a re-entry program assessment. This will confirm that the student is fully capable of living drug-and-alcohol-free and will continue their road to becoming stronger and better every day.

Volunteers and supportive companies run weekly evening seminars on a variety of topics for students who are approaching graduation. These are intended to ease the transition into the world beyond the John Volken Academy, and include such topics as:

- Understanding wants versus needs

- Making and following budgets

- Re-establishing credit

- Finding healthy housing

- Buying a cell phone

- Writing a resume

- Doing online job searches

- Developing job interview skills

Once the JVA program is completed—typically in twenty-four to twenty-eight months, the longest after five years, it's time to celebrate graduation. It is a bi-annual event filled with family members, friends, honored guests, testimonials, laughter, expressions of hope, tears of gratitude from parents, and a lavish buffet and socializing.

Graduations are usually attended by about 200 people with a dozen more on the stage, positioned beneath blue and gold balloons and a giant banner that reads: CONGRATULATIONS. Those on the stage include John and Chawna Volken and six graduating JVA students. Those on the floor include forty or so current students, plus scores of friends, families, invited guests, and supporters. The students on the floor stand facing the crowd and in loud unison repeat The Student Promise, the vow they've been saying twice daily since their first days at the academy many months before. "My life was out of control. My addiction was controlling me. I had the choice to continue on my path of self-destruction or change and rebuild my life. I chose to change."

A graduating young woman stands and says before tears overwhelm her, "There was a night I almost died. I knew I had to change—or die."

A father says of his graduating, twenty-eight-year-old son, "He'd quit the academy. He arrived home one day, stood in the door, and told me he'd left. He couldn't take it anymore, and he was homeless. He promised to never use again. But I'd heard that many times before. Could he take a shower? The answer was, 'Yes, but then you'll have to leave.' I knew he was at death's door. I knew he had to graduate or he'd be dead. And here he is—graduating!"

A young man sporting a bow tie stands and says, "I look at my past life. And look at my present life. And I want to thank my family for not giving up on me."

A mother says she came to the John Volken Academy one day months earlier and saw her son looking neat, working in the store, happy. And she began to cry. Her son came up and asked, "Why are you crying?"

"Because I've got my son back," she told him.

Be grateful and count your blessings. Feeling and communicating gratitude will help you to be more positive, healthier, and enable you to overcome an impulse for something you want now. It supports the recovery process.

And then John Volken stands at the microphone and tells the famous, oft-told story about the Cherokee chief and the two wolves:

> There's this old Indian chief sitting with his grandson, who notices his grandfather's expression. "What's on your mind?" the boy asks his grandfather.
>
> "Oh, there's a terrible fight going on inside me—between two wolves. Each one wants to dominate the other. One wolf is bad—full of insecurity and resentment, lazy and vengeful. The other is good—full of hope, humble, compassionate, hardworking, honest . . ." With that, the grandfather was quiet.

After a while, the grandson asks, "Grandfather, which wolf is winning?" The grandfather replies, "The one I am feeding."

John gives his last advice to his graduates: "We all have these two wolves in us. Before making any decision, think about which wolf is whispering to you. Every small decision we make will lead into bigger ones . . . and reaches into the eternity.

John says to his students, both those on the stage graduating and those in the audience. "Change isn't easy. Nobody wants to be here. But you do want to be here because you know you need to be here."

John reflects:

When a student first walks through that door, no matter how bad they look, no matter what their past is, I love them. It takes enormous courage and commitment to take that first, so-important step to change. Especially for young men and women weakened by their substance abuse. The average drug addict out there insists, "I can quit anytime." Others would rather be in jail—it's easier than changing. They've been feeding the bad wolf for a long, long time. But deep down, they're good young men and women. They are fighting it—they want to change. There is a light in all of them—it is simply covered with this toxin. At the John Volken Academy we understand this, and we love them. All we do is help them to take the toxin out of them and watch the light shine through. It makes it all so worth it.

Susan Richards de Wit, the chairperson of the Surrey, BC, John Volken Academy, tells her story:

What amazes me most is the transformation of the students at the John Volken Academy. They arrive there when they are at a very low point in their lives, but it is not long before the physical and emotional changes begin to emerge. It's truly amazing to observe. John gives them a fresh start in life! Forgiveness and honesty are major components of recovery, and John demonstrates forgiveness to his students directly. For example, during an encounter group session, a student asked John if he remembered the time when his store was broken into and robbed of three TV sets. Oh yes, even though it had been years, John remembered. In the meantime, this young thief wanted to change his life and enrolled in the John Volken Academy. Amid thirty other students he con-fessed that he was the one who broke into the store and robbed it. What does John do? He stands up, walks over to this young man and hugs him and tells him that he loves him for his honesty and courage! That's forgiveness. It's an amazing journey back to an honorable life!

The JVA follows up on its former students for at least six months after their departure. The success rate for JVA students is the highest in the industry, and graduated students continue to go on to university, get married, re-join their churches, start their own businesses—the transfor-mations are nothing short of a miracle. Many times, students who never went to church now want to go. It seems that when the addiction is gone, it leaves a vacuum, which is replaced by the spiritual.

If you look at addiction as an iceberg, that very little tip you see is the drug and alcohol use. But everything underneath—the stuff unseen—is the trauma and the struggle that the addicts have endured. John's life was not without trauma and struggles. Losing his father. Living in East Germany. Alone at fourteen in West Germany. Being an immigrant at eighteen. Starting businesses. These all involved struggles, but he came out on top.

He understands the struggles his students go through; he has lived with them for about twenty years. "They stumble and get up again and again. At the end, they too end up at the top—everyone in their own way. It is so gratifying to witness the journey to success!" But John is quick to point out that he only helps—his students must do it for themselves.

"You cannot do it alone—But you alone must do it."

ENDORSEMENTS

Dr. Faranak Farzan:

"John Volken has truly been a visionary in recognizing the value that transdisciplinary research initiatives can have for helping individuals recover from addiction . . .His early recognition of the need for this paradigm shift is exemplary and provides a road map for other initiatives to follow."

Faranak Farzan, PhD, professor and chair in Technology for Youth Addiction Recovery; director of the Centre for Engineering-Led Brain Research; and platform lead for Canadian Biomarker Network in Depression.

Dr. Evan Wood:

"The John Volken Academy is one of the best examples of drug rehabilitation principles in action."

Evan Wood MD, PhD, ABIM, FRCPC, is a professor of medicine, director of the BC Center for Substance Use (BCCSU), and co-author of over 400 scientific papers on drug policy and treatment. He is a recipient of the British Physician of the Year Award for his ground-breaking research on drug addictions.

David Berner:

"I have been around recovery for fifty-three years and the John Volken Academy program is one of the best. . ."

David Berner is widely recognized as a leading voice on drug and alcohol treatment methodology in the USA. and Canada. Currently, he is the executive director of the Drug Prevention Network of Canada. He has, in a word, seen it all.

Accredited
JOHN VOLKEN ACADEMY
•ADDICTION RECOVERY CENTRE•

The John Volken Academy has been fully certified by the Commission on Accreditation of Rehabilitation Facilities (CARF), the leading international authority for addiction rehabilitation programs. Endorsement by CARF is much more than a certificate on the wall. It is only awarded to drug and alcohol addiction facilities that provide excellent service and constantly achieve superior results.

2001: This duplex on Cambie St. in Vancouver BC was the first John Volken Academy. At that time, the name was Welcome Home.

Left: Vancouver, BC. Oct. 21, 2014
His Holiness the Dali Lama
honored the founder
John Volken with the
Dalai Lama Humanitarian Award
for effectively changing lives.

April 24, 2015: The official opening of The John Volken Academy in Surrey, BC
From Left: Deepak Chopra, Mayor Linda | Emcee'ed by Chris Gailus, News Anchor, Global
Hepner, John & Chawna Volken | BC, made the ceremony perfect.

Three World-Class Addiction Treament Centres

Gilbert, AZ

Kent, WA

Surrey, BC

For more information or admission
One Toll-Free number 1-855-592-3001

Life at the John Volken Academy

Life at the John Volken Academy

The John Volken Academy Farm, 108 Acres, Langley BC.
Under Construction (2021), scheduled to be fully operational in 2024.
Bison • Water Buffalo Dairy • Pigs • Poultry • Organic Gardens •
Orchards • Cheese Processing • Ice Cream • Farmers Market

Eleven of these moving "Beauties" (between Washington, Arizona
and British Columbia) help our students become effective and valuable
employees. The 5-star rating on social media is proof that our competitive
rates and unmatched customer service make us a popular choice for people on
the move, which in turn increases self-esteem of our students. As a social en-
terprise, the moving business also contributes to the financial health of the
John Volken Academy. It is a win-win situation.

CHAPTER 14

STUDENT STORIES FROM DESPAIR—TO HOPE—TO SUCCESS
There Are Hundreds of Similar Letters on File

Martin Smith's Story

He believed he'd reached the end. His story included more detox facilities than he could count on the fingers of both hands—places all across the American Southwest that had offered addiction treatment and the possibility of escape from his ten years of serious addiction. He'd tried many of them and failed every time. Martin Smith, at twenty-four, was exhausted by his seemingly inescapable cravings. He told himself that this time—after a two-month, 2015 stint in a southern California sober-living clinic—he was going to make it—that he was not going to relapse again. He moved back to his family home in Tulsa, Oklahoma, with the intention of returning to college, getting a job, and starting a new, drug-free life.

But within seven months of these resolutions, he collided with old friends and old habits. As Smith explains, "It always happens. Every addict tells the same or some variation of the same story. Saw some old friends. Saw them once. Nothing happened. Saw them twice. Nothing happened. Saw them ten times. Nothing happened. But on the eleventh time, I used. Shooting meth, shooting heroin, eating Xanax. I was just so devastated by it—my using again, because I'd been doing so well during the months before—that I went as hard as I possibly could. I ran with it.

I used uncontrollably for about two months. I think I was on a mission to kill myself. I felt that after so many relapses and so many burnt bridges and all the disappointments and how shitty things were with my family that, um . . . it was really hard on me. I didn't think I deserved to live anymore. I knew I was on a mission to kill myself."

Smith had grown up in Tulsa in what he describes as a sort of Brady Bunch existence: middle-class, financially comfortable, Irish-Catholic family. But as often happens when adolescents hit fourteen or fifteen, insecurity about his identity, along with bullying acquaintances, and a diagnosis of Attention Deficit Hyperactivity Disorder (ADHD) tipped him first toward over-using—and later trading—prescription drugs. And as drug connections and drug cocktails increased in the following years, he graduated to heroin and meth.

With Smith's ADHD diagnosis came a certain, confusing sense of fear and relief. As he describes it, "It's like, oh my God, it's confirmed: There's something wrong with me. Now I can take this pill, and it will fix everything."

But the pill didn't help his teenage angst or his sense of not belonging, being unconnected, and lacking companionship and love.

"I felt I was different. I kept jumping into different friend groups, trying to figure it all out. Who am I? How do I fit? Finally, I found a friend who did drugs and, of course, I wanted to fit with his friends, so I went ahead and took the plunge, and I found something that made me feel whole. Feel complete. It gave me that safety and security I was always looking for.

"I found Oxycontin. I immediately quit everything else. I stopped playing sports. I lost interest in a lot of things. At first it started off as this recreational social pastime—as it always does. Eventually, it became my sole means of interacting with people or feeling connected. I was always really good in my schooling. I was well spoken and good looking. So I kept this really clean exterior and could use drugs pretty much consequence-free because everything looked okay. And any abnormalities in my behavior, were like, 'Oh, Martin's a teenager. He's just going through stuff, right?'

"That's until I went to a private Catholic high school, until the point in the last quarter of my senior year—I was eighteen—when I failed a series of hair follicle drug tests and got kicked out. Any good reputation I did have was completely, oh . . . it was obliterated. People would say, 'Oh my God! Martin does drugs.' I lost a lot of friends. Girls of interest were no longer interested. It sent me into this downward spiral, a really, really dark, dark place." In shame, he decided to hide away in his room, incommunicado for months. He refused to talk with his family. A former athlete, his weight climbed to 280 pounds. His efforts in the fall of that year to attend the University of Oklahoma ended with a relapse on Oxycontin and his being kicked out of university for drug use. He informed his parents he was an addict. They preferred not to believe him. He got put on Suboxone, a form of drug replacement medication for prescription drug abuse. He soon was selling his Suboxone for harder drugs. His parents were furious. He agreed to go to treatment, but only if they sent him to Passages in Malibu, California, the most luxurious and expensive drug and alcohol detoxification facility in North America. Its thirty-day program promises to "find, treat, and heal the cause of your addiction so you can find permanent sobriety." Its cost: over $80,000 a month. Within twenty-four hours of leaving Passages, Smith was back using—only now he was fixing with heroin and mixing it with Xanax. Daily.

This pattern happened again and again. He moved to another state to escape his drug friends, sources, and compulsions. He used. He entered and left detox. And used. He went back to his parents and got busted for stealing their money. He tried a new detox facility, left, and used.

"I used heroin to drive myself downwards, right? I used it to make myself feel invincible, while also creating all this shame, so I could just perpetuate that use," he says, looking back on a wasted decade. In late 2014, his mother told him about the John Volken Academy, located in Canada near Vancouver. He told her he didn't want to go all the way to Canada. And he certainly didn't want to go some place where he'd have to stay for two years. He believed he could detox on his own. He tried once and failed. He tried a second time. And failed. He heard he'd been accepted into the JVA program, but still—for six weeks—he was skeptical about heading north. He feared going and asked himself, *What if I put two years into the place, and it doesn't work? Then, where am I?* On the other hand, he feared not going because he knew for sure where that would lead.

He decided to give himself the ultimate test. He laid out his substantial drug collection on his bed and told himself he was going to use it all. "If I wake up in the morning," he says now of that evening, "that's a sign from God or whoever, that I need to go. And if I don't wake up, well . . . then that's it. So, I did everything. All the drugs, all together. I blacked out completely and woke up one-and-a-half days later."

Two months after that, he crossed into Canada to enroll in the John Volken Academy and began following the ambiguous path toward sobriety and hope. That was over five years ago. Today he is well and sober. He and his family have healed.

Peter Kinder's Story

When Peter Kinder fell into Seattle's grunge counterculture at age sixteen, he fell hard. He was flunking out of high school, playing in a garage band, had his ears pierced with safety pins, and was smoking weed daily. More critically, he realized that if he took the gas money given him monthly by his well-off parents, he could buy—and sell—pot as a business. *I'm going to take this money,* he recalls thinking, *go to my dealer, give him all the money I have, and tell him to give me a good deal. Then I'm just going to start selling weed at school.* "The first day I started selling I went back to my dealer's place four times. Time after time, after time, after time. I just kept on having to get more and more. That pretty much consumed me. It was, like . . . live fast, have as much fun as possible, don't bother dealing with the consequences sort of thing. I told myself it's all I need. I'm just going to live this grimy life."

After graduation, Kinder got into a community college, but quickly dropped out. He saw his suburban friends head off to university, and decided to move to Seattle's University District where he got a job at Costco. After a Seattle party, he was introduced to a big-time dealer who had an impressive selection of illicit drugs. Kinder tried them all. He soon lost his Costco job, and he describes what happened next: "So I remember going over to the dealer's place after I lost my job. I told him, 'Hey man, like, you're not going to see as much of me, I just lost my job.'

"He's like, 'Don't worry about it. You should just start selling for me.'

"I thought, *Well, I don't know.* I'd sold weed before in high school, but I was like . . . I don't know anybody that wants cocaine and ecstasy and pills and everything all the time.

"He said, 'Don't worry about it. Come back in an hour if you're willing to do it.'

. "I went back to his place in the hour, and he gave me a cellphone, a scale, and a $10,000-worth assortment of everything he had, along with contacts for potential clients. For six months, I was working pretty much eight in the morning to ten at night—people stopping outside my place, or me meeting them on street corners. A lot of money was coming in through me and to him. On a good day, selling various drugs, I'd be handling $8,000 to $10,000."

Kinder was nineteen. And, although he didn't know it yet, the path ahead was heading downhill fast. His longtime girlfriend left him, he got kicked out of his band for arriving high for shows, and his dealer was arrested and sent to prison. These events caused him to reflect: *I've thrown away everything for using and selling drugs. I'm not putting money into any useful things. All I do is party. All I do is use.* "It hit me, like, Hey . . . is this where my life's going?" He soon knew the answer. Kinder found a new dealer, and before long, he had acquired a gram-a-day heroin habit. He'd lie in bed, smoke some heroin, fall asleep, wake up, smoke more, and fall asleep again. He couldn't believe it when his housemate told him at one point that he'd been asleep for three days.

His wayward journeys to detox—all funded by his parents—carried him from California, to Seattle, and onward to Spokane, to Idaho, and back to Spokane. Nothing worked. Usually within twenty-four hours of completing a program, he'd score drugs and get high again. He knew he was near the end of the road. "Pretty much all my friends had written me off. The only people who talked to me were my parents and some extended family members. Everybody else, everybody I grew up with wanted nothing to do with me. They knew I was a lost cause. I told myself something needs to change, or I just need to kill myself.

"So, I phoned my mom and said, 'I need help. I really need your help.' She told me about therapeutic communities and how they work. The

John Volken Academy, there's one in Vancouver, about three hours' drive north of us, she told me. There's another in Phoenix. And there's one in Seattle. It's a long-term—two-year—community-based program. It's the people in the program helping people in the program more than anything else. There's going to be people that are counselors and stuff like that, too. They're the authority figures. But it's really about being in a community, with addicts helping addicts.

"I'd become so detached from having anybody close, any friends, anyone. I told my mom, that sounded perfect for me."

Then he adds, "My mom said, 'I'm really happy you called.'"

Kinder has now been drug-free for three years.

Cathy Pierson's Story

Growing up in Utah in the 1990s, Cathy Pierson had—on the surface—a secure and seemingly comfortable childhood. Her well-off parents were members of The Church of Jesus Christ of Latter-day Saints, and so were many people who lived in the suburbs around her. Life was easy, unless you challenged the codes of behavior that come in a community with a homogenous and firmly held set of values. As she says, "Anything different was judged pretty hard. There was a lot of pressure to fit in." At age forty, Cathy's mother rebelled and broke from the Church. She changed her appearance and started drinking and going to clubs. Divorce proceedings were initiated. Cathy was fifteen when this happened.

Cathy felt angry at the Church and angry at life, and soon found within the counterculture of her community, other young people who found the strictures of their parents' faith reason enough to rebel, too. "We'd go to the mountains," Cathy says of that youthful time, "and take psychedelics. Or have these raves or big parties. There'd be lots of questioning about how we'd been raised. The rules. The judgments. The constraints. It resonated with me—like there's something outside of this box I've been raised in. To even think like that—what's true? What's not true? It's seen as wrong by a lot of people in Utah . . . as evil even. Of course, drugs were an important part of all this questioning."

What began, as usually happens, with teenage rebelliousness, with easily available prescription drugs, and partying, quickly morphed for Cathy into something more dangerous. "My first drugs of choice were amphetamines. They were my friend's, her ADHD medication. She'd give the pills to me because she didn't like their effect. But for me, it was love at first taste! I thought I was better, smarter, funnier—a better version of myself with those drugs. I was a better ballerina; I was a better writer. I had to have them. Basically, I became very involved in the drug black market. By my early twenties, I was buying, selling, trading, manipulating doctors. All the time." Then things began to spiral out of control. When Cathy couldn't find prescription drugs, she'd turn to alcohol, and onward to cocaine, heroin, and shooting up methamphetamine. After a marathon night of shooting up meth, her friend told her, "You're done. Once you start using needles, it's the end of the road for you. You don't have a prayer anymore."

She didn't want to believe it. And a month later, she didn't want to believe she was pregnant.

For the next five years, she did drugs, tried to get clean, fought heroin withdrawal shakes, and sought unsuccessfully to reconcile with her young son and his father in Utah. She was hospitalized for severe pancreatitis and was told she would die if she didn't stop doing drugs. Within twelve hours of hearing that, she was drunk off a bottle of vodka. "I played doctors like violins. One gave me a fentanyl prescription and an oxycodone prescription. I still had my benzodiazepine prescription, so I didn't need to drink so much with these powerful prescription drugs. I was so sick. I couldn't digest my food. I was living on broth and toast and just sick.

"I went to a ninety-day drug rehab program with the best of intentions. I thought I'd be fine. But my addiction, I realized, was a lot bigger than a ninety-day program could cure. You walk out the doors the same person that walked in. Nothing really shifts. Not in ninety days. Like you can learn how terrible your addiction is, but you don't adopt a new lifestyle. You don't actually change your values, your cravings, or who you are. You have to have a radical inner transformation. That takes a lot longer than ninety days." After fifteen years of almost continuous drug and alcohol abuse, Cathy hit bottom with crystal meth. Estranged from her son and his father, trapped in her addictions, and dying from pancreatitis, she knew she had to change. "Alcohol was killing my body, just driving me into the ground. With heroin, the withdrawals are terrible. You really get chained to heroin, really a slave to it. But crystal meth—it just destroyed my identity, like who I thought I was. I was insane. Like voices in my head. I imagined bugs crawling in my hair. I was living in a filthy house and afraid of everything." Cathy admitted to her father how desperate she was to escape her demons, and he informed her of a place in Canada called the John Volken Academy that just might be the answer. Curious, she Googled the name and immediately realized it was a big commitment: two years. That didn't bother her at all. She'd tried everything else. At age thirty-four, she says, "I want to get my life back. I want to have a clean white canvas and start over; to be with my son, who's now almost ten; to build the life I've wanted, but could never have because of drugs." Cathy graduated from the John Volken Academy in 2016 and is a manager at a recovery facility in Utah. She is engaged to be married.

Kevin Coles's Story

"By the time I was nineteen," says Kevin Coles, "I was spending pretty much all of my existence in oblivion. I didn't have any friends at that point because of how destructive my habits were. I was going nowhere, and I really just wanted to not wake up. I was depressed, suicidal. My mom saw me in this state, you know. I was getting ready to go to work, but I was so drunk I couldn't even stand—just falling on the ground— and I think that's when she started to realize I was going to die. She didn't know I'd woken up in the forest a few nights before in just my boxers, with no shoes or socks on, all cut up and my arms full of cuts, didn't have my wallet. I'd been beaten to a pulp. She proposed the idea of me going to a Vancouver treatment center. She posed it as a short-term thing, maybe a few months. I didn't know it was a two-year program. Anyhow, she sold me on the idea and I said, 'Yes.' I realized it couldn't get any worse. Why not try it out?"

Kevin's addictions had started in Montreal with pot at age thirteen. He was—in his words—a stoner—hopelessly obsessed. He soon added alcohol that he'd stolen from his wealthy parents' cupboard. He says of that time, "I didn't want to do anything sober. If I was going to go talk to a girl, I wanted to be drunk. If I was going to go to a party, if I was going to get up and go to work, I needed a little bit of alcohol to calm the nerves and . . . you know, it wasn't long before I was drinking every single day. I was always known as 'The Drunk.' People were telling me, 'You're an alcoholic. You should go to rehab.' I was probably seventeen."

By this time, Kevin had added cocaine to his drug menu, and that meant he needed real money to support this expensive, new habit. To do this he'd shoplift. But he found it was safer and easier to steal from his mother's purse or steal things from her home he could easily sell. Admitting this, he sighs audibly when he adds, "Stealing stuff, you know, from people who love you . . . "

As usually happens with overpowering addictions, it got worse. Kevin's pot, alcohol, and cocaine consumption wasn't enough. So he added sedatives. "Typically, I'd do clonazepam mixed with alcohol—that was the only thing that would get me off. Alcohol alone wouldn't do it. The sedatives alone wouldn't do it. I had to take these things together. Which, by the way, people die from this combination. It's an extremely dangerous thing to have that many depressants in your body at one time."

Not long after this, Kevin hit bottom, and his mother made the proposal that he go to Vancouver for treatment. On the day before he flew west from Montreal, he realized he might never get high on drugs again. Ever. It felt inconceivable after so many years of addiction. So, to say goodbye, he took all his prescription sedatives and washed them down with vodka shots. "I have no memory of the plane ride. I don't know what the mentality was really . . . of me doing that. I could never get enough of the stuff. I felt like I was not going to be able to have any more drugs, so I guess I was trying to get as much of it into me as I possibly could. That was my last drunk."

Kevin has been sober for six years.

The Road to Redemption

Just as the paths through youthful addiction follow a common, painful trajectory, so do the reactions of those who agree to the structure and rules the John Volken Academy enforces on its students. Newcomers, like the four students profiled here—and the 120 or so other students at the JVA—confront a daunting, even excruciating adjustment. With their brain chemistry damaged by years of drug use, their bodies physically depleted, their friendships and family ties often in shambles, their attempts at detox self-sabotaged, they enter the JVA and must then face formidable twin fears: drug withdrawal and the possibility they might not succeed. Between that rock and this hard spot, those who leave the program without graduating find themselves back on the street with all the fateful, too often fatal consequences. However, most students choose to stay and graduate to a successful life.

Of those first weeks, Cathy Pierson says, "When I came to the JVA, my whole first two months, I was miserable. I'd wake up and my heart would sink and I'd be like, *What am I doing here?*"

Kevin Coles says, "I was in a lot of pain, mentally and emotionally and even physically—from the withdrawal symptoms. I was not used to being sober. It's hard to explain. I wasn't used to it. It was high, high anxiety."

Peter Kinder adds, "The length of time—two years!—was huge. I knew your brain gets so damaged on drugs that it screws up your decision-making process, your actions, your confidence. It takes your brain a year . . . a year and a half to reset. I wondered if I could get there."

Martin Smith found, "I felt fear during the first days—for doing things wrong, for breaking the rules unintentionally. I was in a state of panic the whole time. But I think there was more fear about leaving— because I knew what would happen then. These fears were mixed with not knowing what to expect—a combination of, yeah . . . relief, fear, excitement, some joy, sadness. There was a lot going on with me." Once the first few traumatic months of adjustment have passed, the students reported they usually settled into a structured and comforting routine. Their hours of waking and lights out are set. And the hours in between follow a daily routine: eating, classes, work, counseling, physical activity, and group meetings. It becomes critically important to the students that the behavior they learned during their years of lying, deception, anger, and denial are regarded in the JVA's community setting as unacceptable. "Absolute honesty is fundamental to your recovery—secrets keep you sick" is what is taught. People who disobey this are confronted by their peers and are required to listen to—and accept without defensiveness—what's being taught. The students come to understand that they are both the patients and the doctors, the students and the therapists.

They are there to help each other, listen to worries, critique misbehavior, support their classmates, demonstrate their patience, and acquire work skills, life skills, and self-discipline, and through these things, to gradually re-acquire their lost confidence.

After twenty-four months at the JVA, Smith says, "I didn't understand myself until I came here. That place has provided the venue for me to be open and vulnerable, to sit with uncomfortability, and really work through some core issues. I had a pretty horrible self-image: not being attractive, being fat, not being liked, not being loved, all sorts of stuff. The JVA is a safe environment."

After fourteen months, Kinder attributes his adjustment to the academy's daily insistence on accountability. In the jargon of the academy—a pull-up. Misdeeds, angry or aggressive behavior, swearing, breaking rules, impatience, slacking off, these are things that will result in someone saying, "Hey I think this behavior doesn't suit you. I think this behavior is going to be your downfall."

Says Kinder, "No one ever did that at other rehab programs. I'd never get challenged like that. And if I ever was confronted before, I'd lie through my teeth. You get good at lying when you're an addict. At the JVA, you have to own your behavior. You have to say, 'Thank you' when someone pulls you up. You learn humility. That's something drug addicts have a huge problem with."

After twenty-six months and successfully graduating from the JVA, Coles says, "It sounds strange, but one of the things you have to learn is getting used to routine. Before—in Montreal—I'd always be late for everything. I wasn't used to any routine. Working for my father's company, I couldn't get fired because my father was the boss, so I kind of did what I wanted. I wasn't used to having to follow rules. At the John Volken Academy, you adjust to a loss of freedom. You don't go out on Friday nights. You don't go out on weekends. Before, I'd go out pretty much every night of the week. So it was huge at first, not going out on weekends, and blowing all my money on drugs and alcohol, and trying to have the most crazy night possible. At the JVA, you get used to being okay, being sane, going to bed at 9:30, and doing your responsibilities the next day, and just kind of doing what most people do. Being—quote/unquote—normal."

After graduating from the JVA, Pierson says, "What was missing from my attempts at recovery before was, I think, the giving-back aspect. The model of the JVA is a therapeutic community. Addicts helping other addicts. I don't believe you can get better without helping others get better. The idea we're all in it together is really powerful."

She gives an example: "There's this thing called the bench. The bench is a real bench. Students go there when they're having trouble, or if they want to leave. And they sit. One time I was on the bench. I was in tears, I was hysterical, and I wanted to go home. I missed my son. He was growing up without me. *What am I doing here?* I was thinking. *I want to go home.* One of the guys in the program, he sat down and talked to me for a while. At first, he was just trying to kind of calm me down. I was saying, like, 'I feel so horrible.'

"He's like, 'At least you can feel now, you're not dead inside like you were.'

"He stayed with me for an hour. He just heard me out, and just like . . . kind of supported me, and told me his experiences when he was new in the program, and the times he'd wanted to leave. After just crying to him for an hour, I felt heard and understood, and I was like, okay, if you can do it, then maybe I can do it, too."

Drug abuse is wrong – you might say it is evil inspired, because it destroys the soul, enslaves the mind and cripples the body.

WHAT PROGRAM PARTICIPANTS SAY!

In addition to the stories chronicled in this chapter, the JVA has received thousands of letters. Here are just a few excerpts from those letters.

- . . . I went through nine different programs with no success. I literally hoped I would die. The John Volken Academy saved my life! . . . I cannot thank you enough for what you have done in not only my life, but my family's as well . . .

- . . . I was lost and just wanted to die. I had no idea how meaningful my life could be . . . the John Volken Academy has created a new person . . .

- . . . Thank you! Not for saving my life, but for giving me a life worth saving . . .

- When I came to the John Volken Academy I was a complete mess, I could not sit still, nor could I think straight. . . . If I can turn my life around, anybody can . . .

- . . . I have grown significantly . . . I've had to change things about myself that I didn't even know needed fixing . . .

- . . . If it wasn't for the John Volken Academy I'd be lucky to be in jail—I'd probably be dead . . .

- . . . I should have been dead a few times. After failing at seven treatment centers, I found my recovery at the John Volken Academy, the long-term program that works. It literally saved my life . . . Now I have been sober for four years. I am excited about life . . .

- . . . many of my misunderstandings about myself and people have changed so much, I don't know how I could have thought differently . . .

167

- . . . your program has changed me from a lying, drug abusing, criminal to a respectable, trustworthy, happy man. I have found myself, my purpose, good friends . . . and for that I am forever grateful.

- . . . my parents spent over $100,000 on rehabilitation programs. All wasted. The John Volken Academy taught me how to stay sober . . . My parents say it's a miracle . . .

- . . . I weighed 360 pounds, took a handful of pain pills every day, and smoked and drank constantly . . . Now I am a role model to my fellow man . . .

- . . . I contemplated suicide, even held a loaded pistol to my head . . . thank you, thank you, thank you . . . I now have an awesome job and a very happy life . . .

- . . . I drank until I couldn't feel and took pills that made me feel numb. I have been in and out of different treatment centers and nothing has worked for me . . . the John Volken Academy has molded me into the man I have always wanted to be . . .

- . . . my emotions have been treated in the best way . . .

- . . . I have learned to laugh, cry, serve, and so much more. The friends I have made will last a lifetime. My life has been saved . . .

- . . . I would most likely be buried next to my mother in Red Deer. The people, the places, the drugs I abused would have ended my life. My life was so out of control, so chaotic, that I literally lived hour to hour not knowing or caring if death was around the corner . . .

- . . . I truly believe in this program with all my heart, now that my heart is working properly . . . the John Volken Academy has taught me to let go of my past and start a brand-new slate . . .

- . . . I cannot express just how grateful I am for your program. I have grown mentally, physical, emotionally, and even spiritually . . . I know God has a plan for me . . .

- . . . the John Volken Academy has molded me into the man I've always wanted to be. I have learned so much at the Academy; work ethics, communication skills, and leadership qualities, to name just a few.

- . . . I had tried and failed at many recovery centers . . . this program has changed my thinking, attitude and behaviors. I'm a different person. I like myself . . . words are difficult for me to describe how I truly feel about the John Volken Academy . . . I am blessed . . .

- . . . I wish that people who are addicted to drugs and alcohol knew that there was hope and an abundant life waiting for them . . . I tried to get clean for years . . .

- . . . Has it been easy? No. But has it been worth it? DEFINITELY!

- . . . I hated joining a program, but I hated my life even more. All that hate turned into love . . .

- . . . no one thought I'd ever clean up and make something of myself . . . writing this letter is proof that I beat all odds . . .

- . . . thank you for inspiring me, encouraging me, and giving me a safe, positive environment to change and grow . . .

- . . . I kept myself imprisoned and a slave to my addiction . . . I really don't know how I've made it that far . . . thank you for providing a safe and structured place . . . I love you . . . thank you for believing in me . . .

- . . . At the John Volken Academy I have learned how to cope with life's challenges . . . I progressed emotionally, intellectually, spiritually, and socially . . .

- . . . before I came to the John Volken Academy I determined that my life was hopeless and I would die addicted to heroin. My life has not only destroyed me but my family's as well . . . Today I want to preach to the world that true recovery is attainable . . .

CHAPTER 15

MY MILLION-DOLLAR LESSON ON FAITH
Why Does It Take so Long to Learn?

The John Volken Academy program is demanding, but it is effective. It has all the components needed for a graduate to lead a healthy, successful life. This minimum two-year program includes balanced healthy meals, clean modern accommodation, individual and group therapy, job and career training, personal development, physical wellness, education, recreation, mentoring, plus a monthly stipend during the final six months to gain general knowledge in financial matters and the importance of budgeting. After completion of the official program it continues with an aftercare agenda.

So who pays for all of this?

Most of the program cost is covered by social enterprises operated by students of the John Volken Academy. The balance is paid for by donations from private charitable foundations, friends of the Academy, supporting businesses, and parents or friends of our students.

This leads to my million-dollar lesson on faith.

In the past, we required a $5,000 intake or commitment fee for individuals to enroll in the two-year program. This fee was easily justified because my foundation subsidizes the three John Volken Academies to the tune of about $300,000 every month, not including donations and support received from other sources. However, it weighed heavy on my mind when people, who so desperately needed the program, had to struggle to raise the required intake or commitment fee. So we decided to not make this fee mandatory. Now anyone who is unable to afford this fee is invited to apply for a Program Scholarship. We do not turn people away just because they can't afford this fee, as long as the applicant meets the intake requirements such as age, medical and physical health. Of course, without this fee, our financial shortfall would increase, and the hope was (and is) that this shortfall will be covered by donations. This was a leap of faith, but looking back on my life, when I followed similar promptings, it ended well. However, when I ignored these promptings, it more often than not ended in a negative outcome.

Here is my story that will make the point:

During 1994, I thought about selling my furniture business. We made over $10 million profit per year, and in addition, we paid down a substantial amount of the mortgages on the buildings that housed our furniture stores. This financial success was certainly satisfying, but as I said before, the challenge of building a business gave my life more purpose than making money. The money is a (welcomed) bonus, and I had enough of this "bonus" accumulated, not in the bank, but as an investment in the business and buildings. I got ready to sell it all and engaged KPMG to facilitate the sale. Their "professional advice"— was a little-known course of action that would save me about six million dollars in capital gains tax when making the sale. I simply had to roll my Canadian furniture business into a Quebec company—the tax laws in Quebec would save the capital gains tax. All I had to do was buy a Quebec company with at least two employees and a two-year operating history, roll my BC business into that Quebec company, and kaboom—I'd save about six million dollars in taxes.

My lawyers, general manager, the KPMG consultants—in fact, it seemed everybody—thought it was a great idea, really great. Everybody, except me.

I consider myself to be a pragmatic, common-sense type of guy, and my hesitation made me wonder, "Why am I so resistant to this obviously beneficial business deal?" . . . it was legal and would save me a ton of money . . .

Finally, after several months of being constantly reminded by everyone who knew about the tax advantage, I relented. Despite the continual inner impressions not to do it, I gave in to the "pressure" and made the move. I bought a video store in Montreal, Quebec, with six employees and a five-year operating history, so the Quebec business qualified. My younger brother Roger moved to Montreal to manage the newly acquired business and I took steps to transfer my shares in the furniture business from a BC company to a Quebec company. Because the business continued to be more profitable every year, I was in no particular hurry to sell, but I moved forward to prepare for the sale.

I had spent over a million dollars to buy the video store, paid the fees for the legal transfer of the business, paid to move my brother from BC to Quebec, and paid KPMG for their advice and services. I was ready to proceed with the actual transfer of the business when, without any inkling, the million-dollar lesson in faith materialized; the tax laws in Quebec changed, and the "amazing" tax advice from KPMG went "up in flames."

Who could have known? There is no doubt in my mind that the prompting came from above. I would have saved myself over a million dollars if only I had enough faith. Looking back, it is now so clear!

Lesson learned: Having faith also requires actions.

CHAPTER 16

CONCLUDING THOUGHTS ABOUT ADDICTION AND RECOVERY

The most fundamental, but often overlooked, aspect of addiction recovery is that for any treatment to be effective, it must include three essential elements:
- treatment of the **symptom (behavior)**
- treatment of the **cause**
- acquiring the **tools to stay sober**

The Symptom
The abuse of drugs and alcohol, along with other addictive behaviours such as gambling, shopping, or sexual compulsion, is not the cause of an addiction—it is merely a symptom. Not to make light of it, but after a few weeks of abstinence, the immediate craving—the symptom—starts to diminish, and the individual begins to look and feel healthy. But this is only the first step towards recovery. Those who receive just a few months of treatment often end up relapsing because they do not address the causes of the addiction.

The Cause
The cause of an addiction is what drove the person to drugs or alcohol in the first place. It is some underlying issue (or issues) that makes the person unable to cope with life as it is. Unlike the symptom, the cause is often difficult to discover, and takes a great deal of time to be properly addressed. Not doing so will likely result in relapse.

The Tools to Stay Sober

To ensure life-long sobriety, the recovering addict must acquire the ability to handle life's many challenges. They must change their lifestyle, attitude, behaviour, and values and develop the necessary tools to stay sober. This takes time; while practicing healthy living day in and day out, the brain gradually begins to heal and form new patterns to replace old behaviors.

The Brain Needs to Heal and Re-Wire Itself

While there is much discussion about the lasting effect the abuse of drugs and alcohol has on the brain, most experts agree that addiction impairs brain development and function. To better understand the "why and how," it helps to know that the brain does not fully develop until a person reaches their mid-twenties. The last area to mature or develop is the frontal lobe, which regulates the "emotional control center."

The impairment caused by substance abuse is evident in the impulsive, emotional, irrational, even stupid decisions that most addicts make. It is common for someone still active in addiction in their 30s or 40s to have the emotional maturity of a teenager. The brain still functions, but not effectively. Much like a river that has been dammed by a mudslide, the muddy water still finds its way to the ocean. Similarly, the brain's messages, while somewhat distorted, find their way to their proper destination.

The good news is that the brain, in fact the whole body, is an amazing healing machine. When the addiction has stopped, the brain begins to heal or rewire itself. This is known as neuroplasticity. The key here is "itself." No professional can do it. With a relatively short time of abstinence, in the proper environment, and with new patterns of living, improvement in brain structure and function become evident. However, it takes time and consistent practice for the brain to function at its optimum. During the healing or rewiring process, the person's actions, reactions, and decision-making abilities remain distorted, but continue to improve. That can take up to five years of sobriety until the brain is as good as it will ever be; and if the recovered addicts continue to use the proper tools, they will be able to maintain sobriety for life. A critical component for lasting sobriety is for the recovering addict to regularly attend support groups such as AA and NA.

The JVA Versus Short-Term Programs

Why is the John Volken Academy more successful than short-term programs?

There are three main answers:

First—the length of time: For individuals who are not predisposed to addiction and have the determination to get sober and stay sober, a short-term recovery program may be sufficient. However, to expect an individual who is predisposed to addiction and has a history of substance abuse to recover and heal in a few months is simply not realistic. Short-term programs ignore the fact that it takes up to five years for the brain to heal to its maximum health. It doesn't mean that in all cases the healing process takes five years, but it is the maximum time for the healing or rewiring to be completed. Any impairment left after that time will be permanent—at least according to the latest research. That is why the program length for most therapeutic communities is at least two years. It takes time.

Unfortunately, the majority of people who struggle with substance abuse are simply not willing to commit to the needed time. To them, two years or sometimes longer is an eternity. They like to think that they can be cured in a few months. As a result, they usually go from program to relapse to needed program to relapse . . .

Second—The John Volken Academy is not a "quick fix" solution—but rather a program committed to changing lives—**for life.** To change and adopt a healthy new lifestyle is an essential component for life-long sobriety. In a long-term (at least twenty-four months) program, recovery is achieved in a dual process. One, the brain has the time needed to rewire, and two, simultaneously the individuals learn and adopt a healthy new lifestyle without stimulants. Among other things, they learn to deal with consequences, personal struggles, challenges, and criticism. They learn all about humility, forgiveness, responsibility, discipline, gratitude, and honesty. They build a strong character while always striving toward perfection . . . and there is much more on their way to perfection. However, it takes time. Years of living a life of abuse without discipline or self-control cannot be changed in a few short months. And without the needed lifestyle change, the individuals will soon revert to the previous destructive habits, which usually leads to relapse.

We guarantee that when the tools acquired at the John Volken Academy are applied, life-long sobriety is 100% attainable.

Third—the cost: The monthly charge for most short-term programs is expensive. The cost is anywhere from about $6,000 to $86,000 per month. At these rates, a few months of treatment may be affordable, but the price tag for the needed twenty-four months or longer would be exorbitant . . . and that is without the all-important teaching of a healthy new lifestyle included in **the John Volken Academy program.**

So, who pays for this program? The Academy teaches self-sufficiency and leads by example by carrying out several social enterprises. These projects serve two purposes. One: They help to defray much of the cost to maintain the program. Two: Students learn job skills, acceptable work ethics, and discover and develop their talents; in short, they learn all requirements for a successful career. Additional funding is needed and comes from private charitable foundations, friends of the Academy, and supporting businesses. This additional support is needed and gratefully accepted so that we are able to offer the John Volken Academy program to anyone, regardless of their financial status. However, to qualify for the program applicants must be committed to changing their lives, willing and able to participate in the program, between the ages of eighteen to thirty-eight with an obvious potential to become self-sufficient.

Addiction Recovery Is a Family Affair

Parents or close relatives and friends are the main contributors to their loved one's recovery. People in addiction are generally manipulative and impulsive, especially when it comes to avoiding difficulties. They will come up with many "convincing" reasons to leave the program. They may plead with their caregivers: "Please take me back; I am healed," or "I can't take it here anymore." There are hundreds of excuses. Some students experience "new" emotions or feelings that were "numbed out" during their addiction.

Because these feelings are difficult to deal with, students often interpret them as negative, or they think their healing process has stopped and they are regressing. The fact is, they are making progress in their recovery, and experiencing these emotions is a sign of healing. Because positive changes are evident, it makes it extremely difficult for parents and friends to say "no" to the pleading of a loved one to come home.

If students leave before they are ready, they may stay sober for a while, but it will likely only be a matter of time before they relapse. That must not happen. A student leaving before he or she is ready may prove fatal because they often go back to using the same amount they used before joining the program. Now, because the body is not used to it, overdosing may be the tragic result. Doing the difficult thing and showing "tough love" by saying no to the student's plea may be just the thing that saves their life. The answer must be "No! We won't let you come home until you graduate. Return to the John Volken Academy." Caregivers should also notify their friends and other family members to support the misguided individual's return to the John Volken Academy and not offer them any refuge or help in quitting their recovery process.

Finally, addiction is a complex issue to which too many people just throw their arms in the air and sigh. However,

Addiction can be defeated.
Faith, courage, and willpower are fundamental to change.
That is a challenge for anybody,
but to no one is it more of a challenge than for individuals under
the influence.

CHAPTER 17

WHAT'S NEXT?
More Science—More Growth

What's the latest research in addiction treatment? Meet Dr. Faranak Farzan. She's a Canadian-trained electrical/biomedical engineer, who has studied at Harvard University's School for Cognitive Neurology. Her goal is to design systems that understand the addicted brain. Today, she's a Simon Fraser University professor, and she chairs SFU's Technological Innovation for Youth Addiction Recovery program. In that capacity, Farzan operates a new laboratory at the John Volken Academy in Surrey, BC,—with potentially revolutionary implications. Utilizing JVA student volunteers, Farzan is on the cutting edge of finding answers to these questions:

- Can a person's likelihood of becoming re-addicted be assessed?

- Can the brain's natural ability to reorganize itself—called neuroplasticity—be enhanced for recovering addicts?

- And if so, how so?

- Can today's JVA students help design and later control neuro-imaging devices that would achieve this?

In short, can addictive cravings be understood and mitigated by painless, self-administered magnetic pulses to the precise site of the craving? There is considerable evidence that the answer is yes.

This research—called Transcranial Magnetic Stimulation (TMS)—lies at the frontier of the last great mystery of human physiology: How exactly does the brain work? Finding the neurological answer to how addiction works—and how its terrible effects can be minimized—is one of global society's most critical challenges.

Society has largely failed to deal with the fact that drug addiction is a chronic brain disorder that requires long-term treatment. But knowing what exactly works best to overcome one's addiction is still in the making and there are many opinions.

John says, "At this point there is no clear consensus about what the very best road to success is. The fact is that the long-term approach of the John Volken Academy works. Is there a better way? Maybe, maybe not. However, we want to continue to be on the cutting edge of drug rehabilitation."

According to Joseph Fins, co-director of the Consortium for the Advanced Study of Brain Injury, "Most rehab stays are six weeks, often less. But if the brain recovers through a slow process similar to its development, why do we provide just a few weeks of rehabilitation and think that'll be sufficient? It would be akin to sending your third grader to school for half-days of classes for a month or two and telling him he's now on his own. We know that it takes years for a child's developing brain to learn and mature; a similar commitment to the recovering injured brain now seems indicated."

Dr. Farzan's work with the JVA is meant to investigate an entirely new frontier in the neurology of addiction by bridging engineering with medical science. It requires developing mechanisms and computer programs that can precisely assess brain behavior, and then—in time—modify it. "This is all brand new," she says. "We're working with students at the John Volken Academy who've had a lived experience of drugs. Over time, we plan to establish the brain health of everyone at the academy—by regular monitoring of their brain's neurology. We're not changing anything about the brain. We're simply setting a baseline: This is where people are at. And then, we want to see how their neurological patterns change as the students adapt to a drug-free life. We can precisely follow the trajectory of the brain health of this or that individual over time. What works? What doesn't work?"

To illustrate this, Farzan shows a visitor colorful, computer-generated comparative images of the brain's neurology as it's affected by memories, urges, music, and imagery stimulation. Moving colors blossom and fade as real-time electrical synaptic messages hit various places within the brain. "The million-dollar question is," she says as portions of the brain light up, "what does this or that mean? Can we get it right? The great thing that the John Volken Academy is doing is this: Their initiatives will allow us to create technologies that will not only benefit whoever comes through the academy to get addiction recovery, but will also eventually be available for doctors, therapists, schools, wherever . . . so people's brains can be monitored. The idea is kind of like your cardiac, blood pressure health. I mean: 120 over 80 is good. Now, speaking metaphorically, we need to find out what's the 120 over 80 for the brain. Research is moving toward trying to understand through this neuro-imaging what pathway in the brain is broken, and then come up with treatment that fixes that pathway.

"Depression and addiction are like best buddies. They almost always happen together. Seventy-five percent of all depression starts in youth. They get psychotherapy, cognitive behavioral therapy, or antidepressants. These fail to be effective in about fifty percent of youth. It's the same for treating young people's addictions. But if you know the precise neuro-logical target, and if you use repetitive magnetic pulses, you can actually suppress a brain region, or you can facilitate its activity.

"Some early studies have shown that for cocaine and heroin users, this neuro-modulation strategy minimizes drug-taking and relapse. It could work on PTSD. On depression. On other addictions. It could be used at the academy with new students, as the first few months are the most difficult period in their program."

Most JVA students have been baseline-tested under Farzan's program, and most will go through thirty-minutes-a-day brain training in the near future. If the research produces successful results among JVA students, that information will inevitably ricochet around the world. It will further confirm what neuroscientists elsewhere are finding: There is, quite pos-sibly, a dramatic new method to assist drug rehabilitation. (The cover story headline of the September 2017 *National Geographic* reads: THE SCIENCE OF ADDICTION: How new discoveries about the brain can help us kick the habit.)

In the years following the John Volken Academy's Surrey ribbon cutting in 2014—and the simultaneous expansions of the Kent, and Gilbert JVA facilities—John faced a number of challenges. New management needed to be considered. New marketing tactics pursued. New directions explored. As well, John's guiding "Think Big Or Go Home" principle meant that he needed to consider expanding the JVA beyond the three established academies. And with the recognition that came with the JVA's successes, came interest from governments, universities, hospitals, and organizations involved with drug policy. This meant that he could not simply carry on as an energetic, one-man crusader for therapeutic community treatment of young addicts. He would need to build bridges to others—both institutional and political. Just as his $500,000 funding for SFU's chair in Technological Innovation for Youth Addiction Recovery helped establish Dr. Farzan's five-year project, he also decided—again via the John Volken Foundation—to give $100,000 to Vancouver's St. Paul's Hospital Foundation to help fund the BC Centre for Substance Use (BCCSU). This facility does clinical research, evaluates current services and outcomes, supports the training of substance-abuse professionals, and suggests policy initiatives to counter, among other things, BC's epidemic of heroin/fentanyl-related deaths.

Dr. Evan Wood, who is a University of British Columbia professor of medicine, is the director of the BC Center for Substance Use (BCCSU). He is co-author of more than 400 scientific papers on drug policy and treatment. He was, as well, recipient of the British Physician of the Year Award for his ground-breaking research on drug addictions.

Wood points to the John Volken Academy as one of the best examples he's seen of these drug rehabilitation principles in action. He acknowledges that the BCCSU is now sending young physicians and nursing trainees to the Academy to see how it works. And he will, in turn, provide the JVA with drug-therapist referrals and nursing advice for the school.

"You go to the John Volken Academy, and you'd never know the young men and women there were once drug users," says Wood. "You talk to them, you watch them in action . . . and you'd never know."

Finally . . .

Almost sixty years ago, a German teenager set out to chop down trees in the Canadian wilderness. That never happened . . . Neither did he become a sea captain, despite his romantic, youthful wanderlust. Nor did his various stints at selling flowers, real estate, frozen food, insurance, cameras, clothing, and a self-help book become his culminating career choice. Each was, at the time, an education an opportunity, and an adventure. He has never shied away from risk, nor has he ever accepted conventional thinking. When he applied what he learned from these experiences to his United Furniture Warehouse business venture, and to his charitable work during the past twenty years, he never looked back. Recognition and awards followed.

The idea of slowing down or retiring is far from John's mind. "There's no quitting. I enjoy the work and relish facing and overcoming challenges." He recalls a recent conversation he had with eighty-nine-year-old Jim Pattison, his former West Vancouver neighbor, a self-made billionaire. "I asked him, 'Don't you ever want to quit?' Pattison replied, 'I love what I'm doing. I've got something like forty companies. I still visit all of them every year. Tomorrow I am going to be on the plane again . . .'"

John asserts, "Both Joe Segal and Jim Pattison, two of my living business heroes, are about ten years older than I am and are still going strong, so age-wise I still have a long way to go. I am grateful for my health and for the support from so many people. And without question, the longer the John Volken Academy operates, the more its guiding principles and operational procedures will be entrenched."

So, what's next for John? His profound, youthful friendship with James Gans, his faith in God, the dedicated support from his wife Chawna, and his own deeply rooted philosophy of optimism shaped him into the philanthropist and crusader he became. The mention of his slowing down produces smiles and upturned eyes from those closest to him. They know him well. On the drawing board are two or three more locations in Utah and Nevada and perhaps Texas—to add to his three current academies.

Then there is the farm in Langley, BC. Bilhar Koonar and John spent considerable time over several years finding just the right property. Finally, in 2017 they found this 108-acre tract of land about twenty-five miles from the Surrey JVA. It was a perfect place to develop into a farm; and more importantly, it would become a popular place for the JVA students to continue their rehabilitation. The cost for the land was $6,100,000; and the cost for turning it into a functional farm was budgeted for another $10,000,000.

Marc Vance, a friend of the family, operated a bison and water buffalo farm on Vancouver Island. He was the perfect candidate to manage the farm. His dream for his farm complemented the dream John has for the John Volken Academy farm, but he lacked the capital. So, he sold his farm and is now in charge of the John Volken Academy Farm in Langley, BC. His right-hand man is Doran Pierson who has been associated with John for about thirty years. Prior to his involvement with the JVA, Doran worked for John at United Furniture Warehouse as an Area Supervisor. Having grown up on a farm, he became a much-needed addition to the management of the new farm in Langley. Then Dr. Laila Benkrima joined the team. She has a doctorate degree in agriculture and oversees about twenty acres of vegetables at the farm. It is now a perfect team.

To a limited degree, the farm started operating in 2021 but will be fully operational in 2024. It will feature greenhouses, a marketplace, cheese and ice cream production, bison, water buffalo herds—everything that will complete an agri-tourism destination, which is very exciting. However, as the plans have developed, the budget has ballooned from $10 million to over $60 million. Thanks to an excellent relationship with the local credit union, a much-needed line of credit has been established to cover some of the construction costs for the time being. Expensive? Yes, but it will be a showcase as an agri-tourism destination for all of Canada . . . and a perfect home where JVA students will continue to learn and recover.

On the Kent campus, another store is under construction to add a training facility for students. And in Arizona, a women's center opened in October 2019. All three facilities need more transition homes for graduated students, and his "Lift the Children" orphanages in Africa need ongoing support. More real estate holdings owned by the John Volken Foundations must be sold, but John is very much aware of the fact that his foundations have to keep enough of their real estate holdings so that the rental income from these buildings can cover the costs of his philanthropic endeavors and he is confident that all is well under control.

When asked who will eventually take over the leadership of the John Volken Academy, Lift the Children, the two John Volken foundations in Canada and the US, and the John Volken Humanitarian Award, he says, "Yes that is a concern . . . but everyone can be replaced, and who knows, maybe (hopefully) even by someone better than me. I am so grateful for the effectiveness and dedication of our volunteer advisory committee members. They excel in their stewardship and are well and professionally qualified to carry on this responsibility to assure that the work continues to progress."

In the end, it is not what we gave,
or what we did, or what we taught,
or what we changed,
for that, we received the rewards.
We will be rewarded for what we became, because of what we did.

John O. Volken

HUMANITARIAN AWARD

$1 Million
To Be Awarded To Charities That Make A Positive Impact On Society.

When we first traveled to Africa with the intent of establishing large, western-type orphanages on that continent, we quickly learned that the planned undertaking and its logistics would likely turn into a nightmare. Furthermore, there are an endless number of small, struggling orphanages with caring, capable management in place, but with dire financial needs. Learning from that, we decided to change our plans and support these orphanages instead of building our own. It proved to be the right decision.

Similarly, there are countless organizations that strive to improve lives in their communities and beyond. Many of them can use - in fact need - extra funding to deliver the services they want to provide.

The John and Chawna Volken Humanitarian Award was created to support such organizations.

Since the inception of the John Volken Foundation in 1997, we have dispersed well over 200 million dollars to charity, with most of the funds directed to build and administer the four John Volken Academy locations. We are greatly blessed and pledge continual financial support to charities committed to uplift the needy.

In 2021, more than $1,000,000 was shared by the organizations listed below:

2021 AWARD RECIPIENTS

ALS Society of BC
Atira Women's Resource Society
Avalon Recovery Society
Back on Track Recovery Ltd
Big Brothers of Greater Vancouver
Big Sisters of Greater Vancouver
Blind Beginnings Society
Boys and Girls Club of South Coast
City Dream Centre Society
CKNW Orphan Fund
Coast Mental Health Foundation
Cultivate Canada/Sole Food Farms
Dalai Lama Center
Dixon Transition Society
Food Share Network Society
Guru Nanak's Free Kitchen (GNFK)
HepConnect Foundation
Kids Play Youth Foundation
Korle-Bu Neuroscience Foundation
Lift the Children
M2/W2 Restorative Christian Ministries
Mercy Multiplied

Moving Forward Family Services
Nightshift Street Ministries Society
Pathfinders Youth Centre Society
Peace Arch Hospital Health Foundation
Pearl Life Renewal
Police and Peace Officers Memorial Ribbon Society
Rick Hansen - Foundation
Simon Fraser University Mental Health and Addictions
SOS Children's Village BC
Spark Foundation
St.Paul's Hospital Dr. Amin Jarer
Surrey Firefighters Charitable Society
Surrey Homeless and Housing Society
Surrey Road to Home Society
The Centre for Child Development
The Odd Squad Production Society
The Salvation Army Gateway of Hope
The Sur-Del Easy Does It Society
Trinity Western University
Union Gospel Mission
Wagner Hills Farm Society

We invite you to select a charity in the US or Canada that you feel is deserving of financial support. Have your choice apply thru
www.jcvha.org.

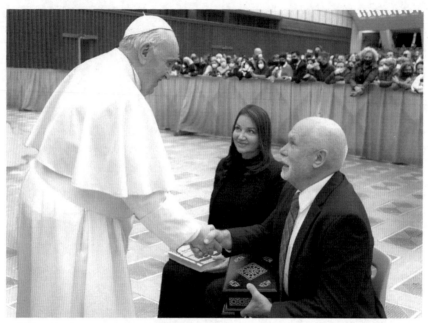

My wife Chawna and I being honored by Pope Francis Dec 15, 2021

We traveled to Italy during the week of December 13-18, 2021, with the intention of meeting Pope Francis. Up to that date, I quietly questioned the reality of the visit. Did I deserve such an honor? The Covid-19 pandemic was also a factor in my uncertanty.

Meeting Pope Francis was a soul-stirring experience. He is the head of over 1.3 billion Catholics and a world leader, and yet, he radiates an almost unearthly humility. No wonder he is so loved, admired, and respected.

By the way, the Pope chose Francis as his papal name, inspired by Saint Francis of Assisi. How intriguing, because when I visited Assisi years ago (page 81), it was a life-defining moment for me. The world would be a better place if we all gleaned even just a little of Francis of Assisi's attributes.

The highlight of the trip, of course, was the two days spent mostly at the Vatican. The visit to the Vatican Museum, featuring the Sistine Chapel, was an event by itself. The museum was closed, so there were only the two of us with a friend, the guide and one security guard. The rest of the week we enjoyed our special time in Rome, all the way down to the Amalfi coast. There is so much to see, and so much to learn.

The Entrepreneur of the Year award in 1995,

the visit by the Dalai Lama in 2014,

and the audience with Pope Francis in 2021,

were some of the highlights of my career.

However, those experiences are just fleeting moments.

Far more important is my relationship with my family,

my relationship with my fellow man,

and above all my relationship with God.

These relationships are eternal.

A huge "Thank You" goes out to our Volunteer Advisory Committee members who donate time, talents and resources, to support the students during and after their program.

The Arizona Team

L-R: Justin Ogburn, Jashin Howell, Rommie Mojahed, Erik Kerbs, Ian Welch, Jennifer & Carson Brown, Chawna & John Volken, Lisa Barnes, Doug Hubbard, Bob Brienholt. Daryl Bethea, Nicole Bonilla, Kyle Conway, Tate Gunning, Curt Brown, Don Stapley, Dr.Brad Barrett, Seth Keeler, Rob Jarvis

The Canadian Team

Back L-R: Bilhar Koonar, Will Phillion, Darrell Hadden, Jamie Fernandez, Gordie Gill, Jane Terepocki, Ian Thomson, Jaynas Prasad, Nav Chhinna, Jon Elton, Dr.Steve Whiteside.

Front L-R: Omar Tahmiscic, Merlin Smith, Abdul Ladha, Jason Watson, Chawana & John Volken, Gabrielle Steed, Maria Cilberto, Sheryl Wong, Chris Szulc, Sherry Marceil, Susan Richards de Wit

The Washington Team

Back L-R: Jeff Burnham, Phil Vance, Randy Klotz, Chawana & John Volken, Jay Bulson.
Front L-R: Julie Shott, Terri Conger, Laurie Bylson, Cameron Smith, Patti & Danny Laronde

Would You Like to Help?

We travel to the moon and back, spending many billions of dollars on weapons that could wipe out all humanity many times over, while at the same time people are starving and others surrender their lives to addiction.

The John Volken Academy and Lift the Children are beacons against the darkness of addiction, hopelessness and starvation.

We invite you to partner with us!

The John Volken Academy
www.volken.org/donate

Lift the Children
http://www.liftthechildren.org/donate

We are a not-for-profit society, so all gifts are tax deductible.
Your donations are very much appreciated.

Thank You!